SPIRIT *of the* CHAPARRAL

The Magnificence of South Texas Wildlife

The Valley Land Fund Wildlife Photo Contest V

Front Cover: Blue Spiny Lizard
                 Glenn Hayes, Photographer
                 Tecomate Ranch, Landowner

Back Cover: Bobcat
                 Hugh Lieck, Photographer
                 H. Yturria Ranch, Landowner

First Printing, 2003
Text and Photography Copyright © 2003 The Valley Land Fund

ISBN 0-9710604-1-X

Published by The Valley Land Fund

The Valley Land Fund
2400 North 10th Street, Suite A
McAllen, Texas 78501
www.valleylandfund.com

Wildlife Photo Contest Office
Phone: (956) 686-6429
Fax: (956) 686-1909
Email: contest@valleylandfund.com

Land Trust Office
Phone: (956) 971-8550
Fax: (956) 971-8565
Email: valleylf@aol.com

Editor: Eryn Reddell Wingert
Co-editor: Ruth Hoyt
Copy Editor: Jan Epton Seale
Printing coordination and color work: Bob Carter, Blue Fusion Design, Boulder, Colorado
Book and cover design: Esperanza S. Chapa, CopyZone, McAllen, Texas
Printing: Gateway Printing & Office Supply, Inc., Edinburg, Texas

Printed in the U.S.A.

Photographer: Derrick Hamrick & Roberta E. Summers / Landowner: A. Cantú Farms

Dedicated to
Alice G.K.K. East and Evelyn East

Alice East and her mother Evelyn are true women of the ranch country of deep South Texas. Their Santa Fe Ranch is managed with respect for all the living creatures in the chaparral. Outspoken and charismatic, these descendants of pioneer ranching families support and maintain some of the most important remaining habitat.

Alice and Evelyn became life members of The Valley Land Fund in 1990 and have made VLF a part of their lives. For more than a decade, Alice served as secretary of the board of directors. Both she and Evelyn have cheered us on in all of our endeavors.

PEOPLE'S CHOICE
Photographer: Randall Ennis & Alberto Gutierrez
Landowner: San Pedro Ranch / Baldo & Danny Vela

About *Spirit of the Chaparral*

The images contained in *Spirit of the Chaparral* were captured during the 2002 Valley Land Fund Wildlife Photo Contest. Photographers spent countless hours in brushland and backyards in the South Texas region between the months of February and June of that year.

Spirit of the Chaparral breaks from the tradition established by the past four Valley Land Fund Wildlife Photo Contest books. The previous editions presented the photographs in winning order by class and division. *Spirit of the Chaparral* offers the winning images in portfolio form.

Grand Prize winning photographers and landowners share their unique experiences from the contest. The photographer's portfolio of winning photographs is subsequently displayed. The portfolios of the remaining winning photographers, the Small Tract Competition, the Youth Photo Contest and the Fourth Grade Nature Photo Contest complete *Spirit of the Chaparral*.

– Eryn Reddell Wingert

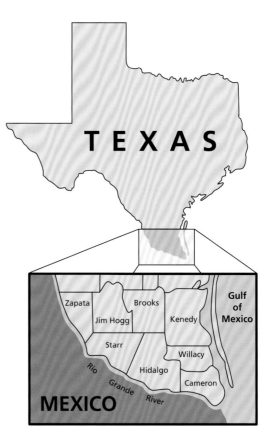

Table *of* Contents

Photographer: Tom Urban / Landowner: King Ranch, Inc.

Preface – *Book V: Spirit of the Chaparral*

Photographer: Dave Welling / Landowner: Pérez Ranch

The animals pictured in this book are descendants of the first Americans. Their ancestors swooped, crawled, and capered over our continent long before humans showed up. This we know for a fact. What do we do with such knowledge?

We act as we should toward any one or any thing that has gone before us on the path of history: We humbly learn.

And what do these creatures teach us as we stand transfixed by their forms, colors, movements, instincts? If we will admit it, perhaps the most important lesson is that we share many common traits with these sentient beings. Other than the obvious commonalities of the flesh, we admit similarities in bodily needs, habits, and lately, even thoughts and emotions. And in certain ways animals are definitely superior to us humans.

Another truth, when we consider animals, is that they are vital components of our natural world. That is, they are not merely objects to build theme parks around or to jumpstart cartoon characters. And they are not to be known as just an occasional face peeking out from woods or grass. No, they are deeply intertwined with their earth, water, and sky homes. And they are not to be thought of singly–here a species, there another–but as an inextricably woven tapestry of life manifest in diversity, interaction, and interdependence.

Both in humility and in hubris, we humans acknowledge that our existence would suffer greatly without the animals. Besides the practical uses we make of them, the comfort, delight, companionship, and wonder they provide make our earthly journey infinitely more enjoyable and interesting.

And these other-presences add a necessary mystery to the world. Perhaps more than ever before, we have come to understand that we will never unlock all the codes of the universe. Past the sophisticated laboratories with their breathtaking revelations, the animals stand patiently, testifying to Being. As Thomas Berry, the spiritual ecologist, has put it, "The natural world is the largest sacred community to which we belong."

The photographers of this contest have garnered from the world around us these images as testimony to the marvelous creatures from which we learn so vitally. We present the pictures to show what has been, to testify to the history of local dwellers other than ourselves.

And we present this book, in sober hope, for the continuance of the animals. Neglectful of their presence, we become less human. Living in relationship and reciprocity, we may become nobler.

We must accord them their broad and rightful place. The Valley Land Fund seeks to do that in our special corner of the world. By tenacious effort–holding photo contests, producing this book, raising money for land conservation, teaching our children to be good stewards, involving the larger public–The Valley Land Fund seeks to guard for the animals what is truly and naturally theirs already. Just as the Valley treasures its cultural diversity, so the VLF leads in the cherishing of biological diversity.

The creatures in this book bid us to read the history of the natural world in their eyes. To feel their ineffable presence. To sense and be awed by the spirit of the chaparral.

–Jan Epton Seale and Eryn Reddell Wingert

The Wildlife Photo Contest, a Brief History

In the early 1990s when The Valley Land Fund was searching for money, John Martin began to think lovely pictures were the answer.

He and his wife, Audrey Martin, researched photo contests from around the country to learn more, but they soon discovered none were just what they wanted to develop here. There were, John says, no true contests, where photographers shoot photos over a specific period of time and were judged on a large body of work.

"A contest is when every shot counts, right now," John reasoned. "It's not about going to a file and pulling out images from the last ten years. A real contest puts people out in the field for some time."

Although the Martins wanted the contest to raise money for The Valley Land Fund, the most important goal was for the contest to cut to the very heart of the mission of The Valley Land Fund: to conserve habitat. Formed in 1987 by the Martins and a small group of Valley residents, The Valley Land Fund wanted to preserve the less than five percent of native, undeveloped land that remained in the Valley. They wanted to educate the public about conserving land and encourage private landowners to conserve their tracts.

"We decided that whatever we did, even if it didn't raise a nickel, it needed to be in and of itself a conservation event," Audrey said.

Three components of the contest were determined: 1) landowners willing to allow photographers on their land to photograph wildlife; 2) the photographers themselves; and 3) conservation-conscious citizens and businesses willing to provide the dollars for the prizes.

So John set out to work full-time on developing the contest. He advertised and photographers began to jump at the chance to compete. They wanted the money, but also a chance to gain access to land normally closed to the public and to have their photos published in The Valley Land Fund photo book.

Plans began in 1991, and by 1994, The Valley Land Fund sponsored the first contest with 90 percent of the participating photographers from South Texas. Today 90 percent come from elsewhere in the country and beyond to have a chance at what has grown into a wildlife photo contest that awards more money than any other in the world. More than $150,000 in prizes was awarded in the 2002 contest.

In 2002, they added a small-tract category to encourage owners of pieces of land as small as a tiny yard to conserve what habitat they have.

Today, contestants enter for the same reasons that they did in the beginning, Audrey says. The awards ceremony, cash prizes and participation have all improved, but what has made the contest a success is that it still furthers The Valley Land Fund's primary mission: to conserve habitat.

For many, the contest has become the very symbol of The Valley Land Fund. Every two years, wildlife photographers try their hand at the contest. The book that displays the winners is a hugely popular gift and the awards ceremony is an elaborate social event.

Even landowners and business sponsors that were at first hesitant to participate have become staunch supporters of the contest.

"As these photographers have documented all the unique critters, it has opened the eyes not only of the public, but also of the landowners about what is on their land," John said.

–Elizabeth Pierson

South Texas Shootout

The South Texas Shootout is a challenging five-month contest that consists of teams of private landowners and photographers. The landowner provides the photographer with access to the property, where the contest photographs are to be taken. The photographer's job is to find and photograph species from fifty wildlife classes, including special categories such as Action, Patterns and Humor. From these photos, they create a portfolio of 100 images to enter in the contest.

A panel of three judges awards points to each slide, and the highest-scoring slides compete for first, second and third places and bonus points. The class winners compete further for placements at the division level, where more bonus points are awarded. The five division winners compete for Best of Contest and more bonus points.

At the end of judging, the landowner-photographer team with the most points is declared the grand prize winner and the first place prize money is divided between them. Prize money is awarded through 30th place. The People's Choice award is determined by popular vote at the El Monte awards event.

–Ruth Hoyt

BEST OF CONTEST
Photographer: Bill Carter / Landowner: CM Cozad Ranch

South Texas Shootout

GRAND PRIZE PORTFOLIOS

First Grand Prize

Rolf Nussbaumer, Photographer
Mark Gibbs and Harold Jones, Landowners
Rio Grande Container Game Ranch, Rincon

Rolf Nussbaumer, Photographer
Photo by Ruth Hoyt

Rolf Nussbaumer entered the 2002 Valley Land Fund Wildlife Photo Contest for love. He had met his then girlfriend Karen while on a trip to Alaska. But geography kept them far apart. He is from Switzerland and she lives in San Antonio. They decided the contest could bring them closer together. Rolf thought, "It would be a good thing to enter the contest to get to see her more."

Meanwhile, Mark Gibbs and Harold Jones, owners of the Rio Grande Container Game Ranch, were looking for a photographer to partner with for the contest. With Rolf in Switzerland, Karen made the journey to the Valley to check out the 650-acre property. Mark gave her a tour and she signed off on the land on Rolf's behalf.

Mark Gibbs and Harold Jones, Landowners
Photo by Ruth Hoyt

Mark and Harold knew the property was special when they bought it from the Bentsen family four years ago. Located near Rincon, Texas, in Starr County, the land has three ponds along with hills rising 425 feet above sea level. "On a clear day you can see the mountains of Monterrey, Mexico," says Mark. The once-cleared land had been left to grow for the past thirty years. Now it is primarily used as a game ranch for customers of Rio Grande Container Company. They also open their gates to Valley Boy and Girl Scout troops to visit and work on ecosystem badges.

The land has every native species imaginable, including Badger, Ground Squirrel, Turkey, Coyote, a breeding Bobcat pair and two species of Quail. Mountain Lion tracks have even been spotted on the property. And an eight-foot Blue Indigo Snake was once witnessed during a survey of the land from a helicopter.

Rolf experienced the vast wildlife firsthand for the five-month duration of the competition. "I was in a water blind in a pond, and a six-foot Rattlesnake came to the pond two yards away from me. It was pretty cool to see that." He believes the main issue in nature photography is showing people what they usually would not see.

"I noticed the dedication and interest Rolf had," says Harold Jones. "It was surprising what an interest he took; he stayed out there and it was so hot."

Rolf's commitment paid off. "Of course, I was very surprised. I hoped to come in as one of the first five. I didn't expect winning first grand prize would happen, coming from another country, with no clue about all the wildlife."

Harold remembers the night of the awards. "He was sitting right in front of me in the auditorium, and when they got to the second place, he knew. He just started trembling. He was thrilled."

Aside from winning the grand prize, the experience of this contest has definitely left a lasting impression. Rolf and Karen married in the Texas Hill Country in front of friends they met during the competition. One of his winning photographs of two kissing cardinals served as the backdrop for their wedding invitations.

Harold and Mark have a new-found respect for their land. "It has raised awareness of what kind of treasures we have here in wildlife in the Valley and that it needs to be protected," Mark says.

Rolf Nussbaumer, Harold Jones and Mark Gibbs all plan to participate in future Valley Land Fund wildlife photo contests.

–Eryn Reddell Wingert

Audubon's Oriole

FIRST PLACE, Jays, Orioles & Tanagers

When I spotted an Audubon's Oriole on my landowner's property, I waited at this spot every morning for two weeks. I heard him sing but he never showed himself. Then, he unexpectedly appeared for a photo shoot near the end of the contest. I never saw him again.

Nikon F5 with Nikon 600mm f/4 AF-1 lens,
1/400 sec @ f/8, Fuji Sensia 100

Jumping Spider

SECOND PLACE, Spiders

These jumping spiders love Prickly Pear cacti. The cactus where this spider lived was full of holes. It took a while before he poked his head out of just the right hole to have his picture taken.

Nikon F5 with Nikon 200mm f/4 AF micro lens, PK-13 extension tube and two SB-26 flashes, /15 sec @ f/22, Fuji Sensia 100

Raccoon

THIRD PLACE, Raccoons

Since I never saw a Raccoon during the day, I was forced to spend many nights waiting for them. I often fell asleep only to be roused by the Raccoons' noisy nosy antics.

Nikon F5 with Nikon 600mm f/4 AF-1 lens and two SB-26 flashes, 1/250sec @ f/5.6, Fuji Sensia 100

I loved using my floating water blind when the days were hot; being in the water was a refreshing break from the South Texas heat. This Least Grebe enjoyed the pond for another reason–frogs!

Nikon F5 with Nikon 600mm f/4 AF lens and TC-14E teleconverter, 1/200 sec @ f/8, Fuji Sensia 100

Least Grebe

FIRST PLACE, Rails, Gallinules, Coots, Grebes, Ducks & Geese

Black-tailed Jackrabbit

FIRST PLACE, Rabbits & Hares

Jackrabbits were plentiful in certain areas on the ranch. They rested in the shade during the day. When the temperature soared to over 100 degrees, the Jackrabbits came to the pond to drink.

Nikon F5 with Nikon 600mm f/4 AF-1 lens and TC-14E Teleconverter, 1/200 sec @ f/8, Fuji Velvia pushed

Killdeer

SECOND PLACE, Shorebirds

From time to time, Killdeer came to the pond for a drink. One day, while shooting a Spotted Sandpiper from my floating blind, this Killdeer came to bathe. I barely had time to maneuver myself into a prime shooting distance.

Nikon F5 with Nikon 600mm f/4 AF-1 lens, 1/640 sec @ f/5.6, Fuji Sensia 100

Six-lined Racerunner

SECOND PLACE, Lizards, Skinks, Anoles & Geckos

I usually only saw these lizards' striped backs as they raced around outside my trailer. I noticed the beautiful pink and blue color tones of the male's underside, which gave me the idea for this picture.

Nikon F5 with Nikon 200mm f/4 AF micro lens and SB-26 flash, 1/125sec f/16, Fuji Velvia pushed

Pyrrhuloxia

THIRD PLACE, Cardinals & Pyrrhuloxias

Pyrrhuloxias frequented my pond daily. I did not need any more Pyrrhuloxia pictures. When I saw this little guy all wet with his crest standing straight up and his breast looking like paint brush bristles, I could not resist snapping a few shots.

Nikon F5 with Nikon 600mm f/4 AF-1 lens, 1/400 sec @ f/8, Fuji Sensia 100

Texas Horned Lizard

THIRD PLACE, Lizards, Skinks, Anoles & Geckos

Horny toads remind me of dinosaurs. With my camera directly on the ground, I got as close as I could to make this modern-day reptile look as big and scary as possible.

Nikon F5 with Nikon 200mm f/4 AF micro lens and SB-26 flash, 1/60 sec f/22, Fuji Sensia 100

Buff-bellied Hummingbird

FIRST PLACE, Swallows, Swifts, Nightjars & Hummingbirds

I am fascinated by hummingbirds; we do not have any in Europe.
I was able to use my flashes to freeze this hummer
feeding among the blooming Purple Sage.

*Nikon F5 with Nikon 600mm f/4 AF-1 lens and PK-13 extension tube,
1/200 sec @ f/11, Fuji Sensia 100*

Crested Caracaras

SECOND PLACE, Owls, Vultures & Caracaras

In the morning's first light, I watched as this pair of Caracaras enjoyed their breakfast together. After dining, they shared a dance.

Nikon F5 with Nikon 600mm f/4 AF-1 lens, 1/400 sec @ f/8, Fuji Sensia 100

Raccoon

SECOND PLACE, Raccoons

I counted five Raccoons around my trailer. With the extreme South Texas conditions, most were lean and mean. This guy might be on the thin side, but he gave me a great pose.

Nikon F5 with Nikon 600 f/4 AF-1 lens and two SB-26 flashes, 1/250 sec @ f/5.6, Fuji Sensia 100

A group of Scaled Quail visited me every morning. I considered them my pets.
This pair enjoyed a dust bath in the dirt pile created from digging a blind.

Nikon F5 with Nikon 600mm f/4 AF-1 lens, 1/640 sec @ f/5.6, Fuji Sensia 100

Scaled Quail
FIRST PLACE,
Action

Green Jays

THIRD PLACE, Jays, Orioles & Tanagers

When I saw my first Green Jay, I used at least a dozen rolls of film on this colorful bird. March was the most popular month for Green Jays at my feeders. They did not like to share though and would become quite loud and aggressive.

Nikon F5 with Nikon 600mm f/4 AF-1 lens,
1/320 sec @ f/8, Fuji Sensia 100

Dung Beetle

THIRD PLACE, Beetles

Dung Beetles amaze me with their ability to make a cow patty disappear in no time at all. They land, make balls, roll them to a prime location, lay their eggs inside the balls, and then bury them. The balls later provide nourishment for the young.

Nikon F4 with Nikon 200mm f/4 AF micro lens and SB-26 flash,
1/100sec @ f/16, Fuji Sensia 100

Red Admiral

FIRST PLACE, Butterflies II (Non-Skippers)

I was surprised to see this butterfly in Texas. We have the very same ones in Switzerland. I caught this worldly migratory butterfly on a typical Texas flower, the Mexican Hat.

Nikon F5 with Nikon 200mm f/4 AF micro lens and SB-26,
1/8 sec @ f/16, Fuji Sensia 100

White-tipped Dove

FIRST PLACE, Doves & Red-billed Pigeons

Late one afternoon this White-tipped Dove chased all the other birds away from the feeders. Then he sat on this Ebony branch to guard his prize, which is not typical.

Nikon F5 with Nikon 600mm f/4 AF-1 lens, 1/400 sec @ f/8, Fuji Sensia 100

Common Ground Dove

THIRD PLACE, Doves & Red-billed Pigeons

The Common Ground Dove is quite shy, usually visiting a pond for very quick drinks. Fortunately, this dove came for his drink in the very last light of day.

Nikon F5 with Nikon 600mm f/4 AF-1 lens,
1/250 sec @ f/5.6, Fuji Velvia pushed

Coyote

SECOND PLACE, Humor

While I was photographing from my water blind, this Coyote marked his territory. What he thought was a private moment is now captured for everyone's viewing.

Nikon F5 with Nikon 600mm f/4 AF-1 lens,
1/160 sec @ f/5.6, Fuji Sensia 100

White Checkered-Skipper

FIRST PLACE, Butterflies I (Skippers)

The ranch had a clearing containing these red blooming plants. In the early morning before the flowers opened, they almost appeared to be roses. I was drawn by their beauty, as was this skipper.

Nikon F5 with Nikon 200mm f/4 AF micro lens and SB-26 flash, 1/4sec @ f/16, Fuji Sensia 100

Northern Bobwhites

THIRD PLACE, Turkeys, Quail, Chachalacas

Every morning for three weeks, about ten Northern Bobwhite feasted on the birdseed that I threw out by the pond's edge. They were always together and in constant motion. To photograph this pair together without others in the background was quite an achievement.

Nikon F5 with Nikon 600mm f/4 AF-1 lens, 1/320 sec @ f/8, Fuji Sensia 100

Bee Species

SECOND PLACE, Bees, Wasps, Ants & Other Social Insects

When the Mexican Hats were blooming, the bees provided ample entertainment for me. They flew from flower to flower, collecting pollen on their legs. After a while, they were covered in pollen and barely able to fly.

Nikon F5 with Nikon 200mm f/4 AF micro lens and SB-26 fill flash, 1/15 sec @ f/16, Fuji Velvia pushed

Bullock's Oriole

SECOND PLACE, Jays, Orioles & Tanagers

This oriole really thought the grass was greener on the other side of the fence. With berries everywhere, she hung upside down to reach a particular berry. What a pose!

Nikon F5 with Nikon 600mm f/4 AF-1 lens, 1/640 sec @ f/5.6, Fuji Sensia 100

Cardinals were daily visitors at the feeders. I was watching this female in my viewer when the male appeared. As I only witnessed this exchange once, I felt lucky to capture these lovebirds feeding each other.

Nikon F5 and Nikon 600mm f/4 AF-1 lens, 1/640 sec @ f/5.6, Fuji Sensia 100

Northern Cardinals

FIRST PLACE, Cardinals & Pyrrhuloxias
THIRD PLACE, Birds Division

Second Grand Prize

Sean Fitzgerald & Jeremy Woodhouse, Photographers
Roberto & Fran Yzaguirre, Landowners
Rancho Yzaguirre, Starr & Jim Hogg Counties

Roberto and Fran Yzaguirre's ranch located in northern Starr and southern Jim Hogg counties has been in the family since the Spanish land grant days and is what remains of once vast holdings. The ranch has placed high on the winner's list in previous Valley Land Fund wildlife photography contests and the Yzaguirres have plowed all their winnings back to enhance the habitat.

His pride is visible as Roberto talks about the six ponds and the big lake he built just for the photographers. In this semi-arid land, water is the key to life, and since adding all the water Roberto says there is ten times as much wildlife. "But, how," he asks, "did a turtle get in that lake that wasn't built a year ago?"

This is the second contest that teamed photographers Jeremy Woodhouse and Sean Fitzgerald with the Yzaguirre Ranch. In 2000 they forged a close relationship with Roberto and Fran and were given a key to the gate and invited to occupy the spacious ranch house.

Jeremy Woodhouse is a graphic designer turned professional photographer and has competed in the last four VLF contests. He is constantly amazed by "so many creatures in such a harsh environment."

Originally from England, Jeremy came to the U.S. via South Africa where his love for nature was first kindled. He and his wife, Nicole, live in The Colony, Texas. He spent 100 days on the ranch and shot some 80 rolls of film. Jeremy says that the "scavenger hunt" concept of the contest disciplines the photographer, demanding that he become a better naturalist and broaden his horizons.

Jeremy also stresses that absolute dedication and patience reap the rewards. One day, after two hours of floating in a water blind, following a Green-backed Heron, the bird suddenly struck and came up with a frog – a winner!

Sean Fitzgerald lives in Dallas, Texas with his wife Karen. He stopped practicing law to pursue a career in wildlife photography. He spent about eight weeks on the ranch over several trips. On a typical day he would be up an hour and a half before sunrise to check the weather. If clear, he would sit in the blind before first light and stay as long as conditions were good. Later, he would shoot macros and then return to the blind in the afternoon.

What Sean learned was, "To be in tune with the rhythms of the Valley and realize that the heat, the wind, rain, clouds and insects are all part of the plan; not to be fought, but understood."

Fran Yzaguirre believes the contest benefits the community by creating an awareness of the beauty that is out there. Sean agrees, "It punctures the veil of what's behind those fences and in those thickets. The books and traveling photo displays highlight the diversity and, over time, there is a growing pride, not just in the landowners but in the community."

–Audrey G. Martin

This photo was taken on one of the very few windless mornings.
There was light dew, which added to the patterned texture of the composition.

Canon EOS 1V with Canon 180mm f/3.5 macro lens and 2x teleconverter, Kodak E100VS pushed one stop

Spiderlings
FIRST PLACE, Patterns
FIRST PLACE, Special Categories Division

Sawfly

THIRD PLACE, Bees, Wasps, Ants & Other Social Insects

In June we had a couple of days' respite from the winds, and I was lucky enough to find this wasp covered in dew. - J.W.

Canon EOS 1V with Canon EF 180mm f3.5 macro lens and 2x teleconverter, 1/2 sec @ f/22, Kodak E100vs pushed one stop

Crested Caracara

THIRD PLACE, Humor

This was one of several Crested Caracaras that had been feeding on a Javelina carcass. Suddenly it tossed its head back in the air and began calling.

Canon EOS 1V with Canon 500mm f/4 IS lens and 1.4x teleconverter, 1/500 sec @ f/5.6, Kodak E100 VS pushed one stop

Red-tailed Pennants & Familiar Bluets

FIRST PLACE, Dragonflies & Damselflies

I crawled up to the pond's edge with a beanbag and
my camera to shoot the frogs and the blue damselflies.
The two mating dragonflies landed briefly on the tip
of the branch, then flew away. - S.F.

*Canon EOS 1V with Canon 300mm f/2.8 lens and 2x teleconverter,
1/125 sec @ f/11, Kodak E100VS*

Painted Bunting

FIRST PLACE, Buntings, Grosbeaks & Woodpeckers

After I set up my blind in a waterhole, it did not take the birds long to get used to it. Unfortunately, the noise of the camera's motorwind usually scared them off after one or two frames. - J.W.

Canon EOS 1V with Canon 500mm f/4 IS lens and 2x teleconverter, 1/320 sec @ f/8, Kodak E100VS pushed one stop

Pyrrhuloxia

SECOND PLACE, Cardinals & Pyrrhuloxias

I had set up my perch at the closest focusing distance of my lens to try to get really intimate portraits of birds drinking. This Pyrrhuloxia stayed for one single frame. - J.W.

Canon EOS 1V with Canon 500mm f/4 IS lens, 2x teleconverter and 25mm extension tube, 1/320 sec @ f/8, Kodak E100VS pushed one stop

Great Horned Owl

THIRD PLACE, Action

I had a hunting blind set up near the owl's nest. I had been waiting there for a couple of hours one evening, when the mother flew in, giving me this great opportunity. - J.W.

Canon EOS 1V with Canon 500mm f/4 IS lens and 1.4x teleconverter, 1/500 sec @ f/5.6, Kodak E100VS pushed one stop

Killdeer

FIRST PLACE, Shorebirds

On a quiet morning the silence was suddenly shattered by the shriek of the Killdeer. It walked to within 15 feet of my blind, and I had no time to remove the doubler from my camera. - J.W.

Canon EOS 1V with Canon EF 500mm f/4 IS lens and 2x teleconverter, 1/250 sec @ f/8, Kodak E100VS pushed one stop

Western Diamondback Rattlesnake

SECOND PLACE, Patterns

I had been photographing a spider on a Prickly Pear early one morning. As I was going to leave, I turned to go to the car and noticed this sleeping Rattlesnake coiled up no more than two feet from me. - J.W.

Canon EOS 1V with Canon 100-400mm IS lens, 1/8 sec @ f/22, Kodak E100VS

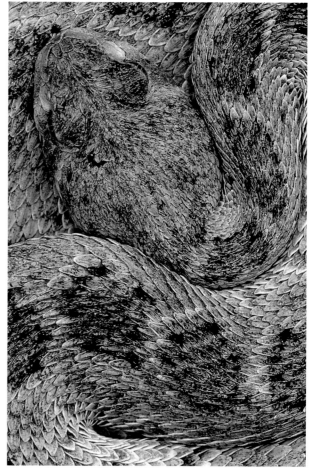

Gray Catbird

SECOND PLACE, Mockingbirds, Thrashers, Catbirds & Thrushes

I photographed this catbird from a dug-in pit blind at water level. – S.F.

Canon EOS 1V with Canon 600mm f/4 IS lens, 1/125 sec @ f/5.6, Kodak E100VS

Texas Horned Lizard

FIRST PLACE, Camouflage/Mimicry
THIRD PLACE, Special Categories Division

I came across this horned lizard on one of the ranch roads. I picked it up, marking the spot, and took it to a sandy, windswept area. As I put it down on the sand, it immediately buried itself. After the picture, I returned it to the place I found it. - J.W.

Canon EOS 1V with Canon 180mm f/3.5 L macro lens, 1/15 sec @ f/22, Kodak E100VS pushed one stop

Moth Caterpillar

SECOND PLACE, Moths

On a rare still morning, I photographed this caterpillar with beautiful backlighting. I elected to bounce in a little fill-flash set at about -2 to bring out the colors in the caterpillar. - J.W.

Canon EOS 1V, Canon EF 180mm f/3.5 macro lens, 1/60 sec @ f/16, Kodak E100VS, pushed one stop

Green Heron

THIRD PLACE, Wading Birds

On an overcast day, I was following this heron in my floating blind. After about an hour it caught a Leopard Frog. Five minutes elapsed before the bird finally swallowed it. - J.W.

Canon EOS 1V with Canon EF 500mm f/4 IS lens, 1/500 sec @ f/4, Kodak E100VS pushed one stop

Lark Sparrow

SECOND PLACE, Sparrows & Towhees

I liked the way the sparrow blended in with the grasses which surrounded the waterhole. It makes the portrait more intimate. - J.W.

Canon EOS 1V with Canon 500mm f/4 and 2x teleconverter, 1/320 sec @ f/8, Kodak E100VS pushed one stop

Green Lynx Spider

THIRD PLACE, Spiders

It had been drizzling off and on all morning. I photographed this spider as it hunted around cacti. - S.F.

Canon 1V with Canon 180mm macro lens, 1/90 sec @ f/11, Kodak E100VS

Western Meadowlark

FIRST PLACE, All Other Birds

During migration in early February, this was one of a flock of meadowlarks which passed through in two days. The backlighting provides the mood in this image.

Canon EOS 1V with Canon 500mm f/4 IS lens and 1.4x teleconverter, 1/125 sec @ f/5.6, Kodak E100VS pushed one stop

Third Grand Prize

Larry Ditto & Greg W. Lasley, Photographers

Bud & Jimmy Payne, Landowners

Payne Ranch, Encino

Larry Ditto and Greg W. Lasley both took up photography in the 1970s, while serving in the military. Larry picked up a camera in Vietnam and when he returned home, almost immediately began photographing wildlife. Greg started out documenting rare papers and later, unusual birds. The rest is history.

They first teamed up in the 2000 Valley Land Fund Wildlife Photo Contest. It was Greg's first contest and Larry's fourth time in the South Texas Shootout. Both retired, Greg from the Austin Police Department and Larry as a refuge manager, they devoted days on end to photographing on the Payne Ranch. Their efforts resulted in a First Grand Prize win. During the recent competition, they secretly hoped to make Valley Land Fund photo contest history. "I was perfectly happy, obviously, with the 2000 contest. And I'm perfectly happy with the outcome of 2002," says Greg. "We kind of, in the back of our minds, hoped to win twice."

Garnering the Third Place title provided rewarding experiences for the two photographers. "The most meaningful thing for us is the awareness for the owners," says Larry, "and the remoteness of it, what early ranchers must have gone through to live out there."

The Payne Ranch is owned by Bud Payne, his wife Marlee and brother Jimmy. Located fifteen miles from Encino, the 7500-acre property sits in a "great neighborhood," claims Bud. The ranch is bordered by the King Ranch, the Armstrong and the Santa Fe ranch. Bud declares, "It's my place, my heart."

The land is used for cattle, hunting and recreation and offers a broad range of unique habitat. The Paynes' guiding principle concerning the land is enhancement of wildlife. Being a part of four out of the five photo contests plays a big part in that principle. "The thing that interests us the most is being able to share our ranch and public awareness of the absolute gifts the Valley has in the natural habitat," states Bud.

The Valley Land Fund Wildlife Photo contest certainly offers a good forum to share and reveal nature. According to Larry, it's one of the best conservation tools in the Valley. "The photo contest and all the attention that surrounds it have made a major impact on conservation and especially on the landowners," he states.

Greg and Larry have made an impact of their own on the Paynes, some memories a little more lasting. "The thing I still laugh about in my dreams is seeing 6-foot-8 Larry in a tube in about a six-inch pond of water," exclaims Bud. But despite that lasting impression, Bud adds, "I feel like they are dear friends now. There couldn't have been a better experience for Marlee, Jimmy and me."

–Eryn Reddell Wingert

Wild Turkey

FIRST PLACE, Turkeys, Quail & Chachalacas

As the gobbler fed toward my blind, he began a "running stretch" that included several wing flaps. I was fortunate he passed a Prickly Poppy flower as I shot several frames of the action. - L.D.

Canon EOS 3 with Canon 500mm and 1.4x teleconverter, 1/500 sec at f/5.6, Fuji Velvia

Scissor-tailed Flycatcher

FIRST PLACE, Flycatchers & Kingbirds

A pair of Scissor-tails were feeding their young in a treetop nest.
The adults displayed, then scolded the photographer.

Canon EOS 3 with Canon 500mm lens and 2x teleconverter, 1/250 sec @ f/8, Fuji Velvia

Buff-bellied Hummingbird

THIRD PLACE, Swallows, Swifts, Nightjars & Hummingbirds

Cactus flowers don't offer much food for hungry hummingbirds, but this bloom opened a few minutes before the bird's arrival, and it was the only available flower in sight.

Canon EOS 3 with Canon 500mm f/4 IS lens and 1.4x teleconverter, 1/180 sec at f/8, Fuji Velvia

Coyote

SECOND PLACE, Coyotes & Foxes

I had been in a blind watching vultures on a carcass when this Coyote came prancing up. I was lucky to catch a shot of him as he licked his chops. The cactus spine in his right ear adds a special touch. - G.L.

Canon EOS 1V with Canon 500mm f/4 and 2x teleconverter, 1/250 sec @ f/8, Fuji Velvia

Northern Mockingbird

THIRD PLACE, Mockingbirds, Thrashers, Catbirds & Thrushes

Pausing atop a clump of ball moss to "check out" the situation, the Mockingbird dropped to a small puddle for his morning bath.

Canon EOS 3 with Canon 500mm f/r IS lens and 1.4x teleconverter, 1/200 sec @ f/5.6, Fuji Velvia

Familiar Bluet

THIRD PLACE, Dragonflies & Damselflies

On a June morning with heavy dew, I found a number of damselflies perched on weed stalks. This one seemed especially photogenic, showing the dew drops on its back. - G.L.

Canon EOS 1V with Canon EF 70-200mm f/2.8 lens with close-up filter and flash, 1/60 sec at f/16, Fuji Velvia

Cassin's Sparrow

FIRST PLACE, Sparrows & Towhees

Cassin's Sparrows were common singers on the Payne Ranch, but difficult to photograph. I spent many hours one day in April trying to get photos of this singing male. Finally, he accepted me near his favorite song perch. - G.L.

Canon EOS 1V with Canon 500mm f/4 IS lens and 2x teleconverter, 1/250 sec at f/8, Fuji Velvia

Javelinas

THIRD PLACE, Javelinas

Squabbling over the same bite of food is a common occurrence when members of the herd come nose-to-nose during a feeding session.

Canon EOS 3 with Canon 500mm f/4 IS lens, 1/250 sec @ f/4, Fuji Velvia

It is unusual to see salamanders away from water. This one is crawling over surface vegetation at the edge of a pond that was teeming with adult and larval specimens of his species.

Canon EOS 3 with Canon 180mm macro lens, 1/90 sec @ f/11, Fuji Velvia

Barred Tiger Salamander
FIRST PLACE, Salamanders & Sirens

Barred Tiger Salamanders

FIRST PLACE, Animal Babies

In the larval form, Barred Tiger Salamanders have long, fringed external gills that give the appearance of Aztec dancers in ceremonial attire. I believe this side and front view give an unusual glimpse of their underwater activity. – L.D.

Canon EOS 3 with 28-85mm zoom lens, 1/50 sec @ f/11, Fuji Provia

Javelina

SECOND PLACE, Javelinas

The last rays of sunlight hit this Javelina's face as he walked out of the evening shadows and paused to yawn. I shot two frames at very slow speed; one was blurred and one was "tack" sharp. Even with his teeth showing, this lazy fellow was not intimidating. - L.D.

Canon EOS 3 with Canon 500mm f/4 IS lens, 1/30 sec at f/4, Fuji Velvia

Long-billed Dowitcher

THIRD PLACE, Shorebirds

Just after sunrise, this dowitcher paused from his probing of the pond bottom to scratch. This photo was taken from ground level at the pond's edge.

Canon EOS 3 with Canon 500mm IS lens and 2x teleconverter, 1/90 sec @ f/8, Fuji Velvia

Raccoon

FIRST PLACE, Raccoons

Soaking wet from the heavy morning dew, this Raccoon emerged from the tall grass near the edge of a marsh where I had placed a blind. Curious and cautious of the unusual object, he stood up to get a better view, and I had the pose I wanted. - L.D.

Canon 1N with Canon 500mm f/4 IS lens and 2x teleconverter, 1/90 sec @ f/8, Fuji Velvia

Fourth Grand Prize

Tom Urban, Photographer
King Ranch, Inc., Landowner
Encino Division, Encino

Tom Urban has lived on the King Ranch so long the animals have come to know him. He has spent the past 25 years exploring and working the same 20,000 acres.

To capture an image of two bucks fighting at sunset Tom was "in the right place at the right time," he says. One day at dusk, he stepped out with camera in hand to photograph Javelinas, when a herd of deer spotted him and came closer. Tom saw two bucks fighting and took his shot. "It was partly a matter of being at the right place to work something else, and then this beautiful sunset comes along," he states.

Tom began casually taking photographs when he was younger. When he was a student at Texas A&M University, he took photographs for an environmental interpretation class and found he enjoyed it. Now he considers himself a "serious amateur."

He lives year-round in a restored cowboy camp on the ranch, which he likens to some of the nation's most magnificent parks. "This is pretty much wild, untamed country," he shares. "It doesn't have the splendor of Yosemite or the giant Redwoods, but the amount of biomass outshadows all the others."

Tom has helped document years of wildlife on the King Ranch. "Tom's photos, which will be featured in an upcoming book celebrating the ranch's 150th anniversary, have reminded employees and visitors of the fabled ranch about the beauty of nature," says Paul Genho, Vice President and General Manager of the King Ranch. "Entering the photo contest has always been Tom's idea, and the King Ranch has always happily gone along with the idea," Genho states.

The Valley Land Fund contest and other photography contests are valuable because they bring nature to a largely urbanized country filled with people who spend most of their time indoors. "They drive from their offices in their air-conditioned cars while there's a real world out there, and we are still living in that world," says Genho. "Anything that heightens awareness of what's out there is valuable."

Tom plans to continue with The Valley Land Fund photo contests. In fact, he wouldn't mind seeing the already grueling competition turn into a full-year race so he could capture all seasons.

He considers nature photography an art, based on work as much as luck, "as any participants in The Valley Land Fund contest will attest," he says. "You can take a picture or you can make a picture, and most of these people, they have made their shots."

— *Elizabeth Pierson*

As with many reptiles, the Checkered Garter Snake can be difficult to observe. This little snake was coiled up inside the empty shell of a Red-eared Slider. The shell provided protection from hungry predators as well as shade from the hot sun.

Canon F-1 with Canon 80-200mm f/4 L lens and extension tube, 1/60 sec @ f/4, Kodak E100VS

Checkered Garter Snake

FIRST PLACE, Non-venomous Snakes I
SECOND PLACE, Reptiles & Amphibians Division

Eastern Screech-Owl

FIRST PLACE, Owls, Vultures & Caracaras
SECOND PLACE, Birds Division

I had observed a screech owl perching consistently on the same mesquite limb daily. To achieve eye-level composition, I set up a sixteen-foot scaffold blind one night. The next day, when the light was right, I was set to shoot.

Canon EOS 3 with Canon EF 300mm f/2.8 lens and 1.4x teleconverter, 1/100 sec @ f/4, Kodak E100VS

White-tailed Deer

SECOND PLACE, Sunrise / Sunset

Henry David Thoreau said, "We need a touch of wildness." People's emotional affinity to wildness means that if we continue to lose wildlife and habitats we are threatening our mental well-being. The conservation of our natural resources is essential to our psychological health.

Canon EOS 3 with Canon 300mm f/2.8 L IS lens, 1/400 sec @ f/2.8, Kodak E100 VS

Greater Roadrunner

SECOND PLACE, Cuckoos, Anis & Roadrunners

This was one of a pair of roadrunners kept busy feeding a nest of five young. Prey that I observed brought in included grasshoppers, a kaytidid, a centipede, Keeled Earless Lizards, Texas Horned Lizards, Texas Spiny Lizards, Prairie-lined Race Runners and Ground Skinks.

Canon F-1 with Canon FD 400mm f/2.8 lens and 1.4x teleconverter, 1/125 sec @ f/4, Fuji Velvia

Western Diamondback Rattlesnake

THIRD PLACE, Venomous Snakes

A Western Diamondback coiled at the top of an old tree stump fixed its unblinking gaze on me. I was trying to catch the rainbow and rattler with a wide-angle shot. My camera position is about two feet from the snake.

Canon F-1 with Canon FD 20-35mm f/3.5 L lens and Vivitar 2800 flash, 1/60 sec @ f/3.5, Kodak E100VS

White-tailed Deer

SECOND PLACE, Deer

The aesthetic value of a fine white-tailed buck cannot be measured. The wild spirit of the brush country has evolved due in part to these magnificent animals.

Canon EOS 3 with Canon 300mm 2.8L IS lens and 1.4x teleconverter, 1/100 sec @ f/4, Kodak E100VS

A pair of plucky Javelinas was checking each other out. Although Javelinas are well-equipped to fight, they tend to duck for safety when threatened. Barking (like coughing sounds) and bluffing are often used rather than actual fighting.

Javelinas
FIRST PLACE, Javelinas

Canon EOS 3 with Canon 300mm f/2.8 lens, 1/200 sec @ f/2.8, Kodak E100VS

White-tailed Deer

SECOND PLACE, Action

These two deer were really getting a kick out of each other. They were doing the Texas two-step! The bigger deer was leading, while in the background, another deer was waiting his turn for a touching rendezvous.

Canon EOS 3 with Canon 300mm f/2.8 L IS lens, 1/100 sec @ f/2.8; 1/100, Kodak E100VS

Western Ribbon Snake

SECOND PLACE, Non-venomous Snakes I

Ribbon snakes are found around ponds, resacas and streams. In searching for prey such as frogs and small fish, they glide gracefully across the water's surface. They are agile climbers and can be found basking in shrubs.

Canon F-1 with Canon 400mm f/2.8 L lens and Canon 1.4x teleconverter, 1/125 sec @ f/4, Kodak E100VS

Moth Caterpillar

FIRST PLACE, Moths

A tiny inch-long caterpillar was slowly making its way on a bromeliad flower. These "micro" critters are an important source of food for many animals, as well as playing a critical role in the pollination and perpetuation of flowering plants.

Canon F-1 with Canon FD 80-200mm f/1.4 lens and Canon extension tube FD25, 1/125 sec @ f/4, Fuji Velvia

Wrinkled Grasshoppers

SECOND PLACE, All Other Insects

Photographing insects such as grasshoppers will test the tenacity of most nature photographers. In getting eye-level composition with this pair of grasshoppers, I got to enjoy the funny feel of sandburs and the gritty taste of blowing sand.

Canon F-1 with Canon FD 80-200mm f/1.4L lens and FD-25 Canon extension tube, 1/125 sec @ f/4, Kodak E100VS

Black-bellied Whistling-Duck

SECOND PLACE, Rails, Gallinules, Coots, Grebes, Ducks & Geese

In the waning moments of sunset a Black-bellied Whistling-Duck calls out to its mate. The pair has just arisen to roost in a motte of Live Oak trees. These ducks seem to be as comfortable sitting on tree limbs as paddling around a water pond.

Canon F-1 with Canon FD 400mm f/2.8 lens and 1.4x teleconverter, 1/125 sec @ f/4, Kodak E 100VS

Little Blue Heron

SECOND PLACE, Wading Birds

The Little Blue Heron was looking for prey such as fish, insects and amphibians, and the Red-eared Slider was basking in the warm springtime rays. Competition on an old weathered log can have its moments.

Canon EOS 3 with Canon EF 300mm f/2.8 lens and 1.4x teleconverter, 1/200 sec @ f/4, Kodak E100VS

Fifth Grand Prize

Bill Draker, Photographer
Tecomate Ranch Partners, Landowners
Tecomate Ranch, Hidalgo, Jim Hogg, Starr Counties

Bill Draker doesn't think the Tecomate Ranch in northwest Starr County has changed one bit, at least not since 1996. He's spent many hours photographing the ranch since then, most of the time as a contestant in The Valley Land Fund photography contests. The Kerrville resident and retired railroad conductor says with confidence he's seen every area of the ranch visible to the human eye.

"In that time, I think I've covered every square inch of that land," Bill says. "The number of critters is unbelievable. If people don't go out in that part of the country, they just cannot believe the number of critters."

The ranch is largely desert land and becomes unbearably hot for a photographer waiting in a photo blind. This year Bill spent 113 patient days on the ranch and shot 200 rolls of film. One of those weeks in mid-May his camera broke and ruined 28 rolls of film. "You don't even want to know what I thought then," he states.

Bill got into nature photography in 1971 when he took a point-and-shoot camera on a trip to Alaska. When he returned and saw how the wildlife photos developed, he decided he needed more equipment for his new hobby. "I've been upgrading ever since," he claims.

Working alone and at times with a partner, he entered and won awards in The Valley Land Fund Contest in 1996, 1998, 2000 and 2002. The Tecomate became more familiar to him with every visit, but still there are surprises. This year, he was in the right place when a Vermilion Flycatcher came along to feed its young. "The secret to the photos," Bill says, "is a lot of patience and many, many hours."

Bill hopes this ranch and others remain as they are to allow more people to enjoy wildlife. "That ranch doesn't change, not one bit," Bill said. "I hope these places stay like that, too."

In a way, Bill's photographs have already frozen the land in time. Dr. Gary Schwarz, an oral surgeon who owns the ranch with his partners, claims Bill's photos give him the luxury of appreciating the beauty of his ranch when he becomes too busy to spend a lot of time on the land. "It helps me because, seeing it through that lens, there's a beauty there," Schwarz says. "Those photographs are a way of forcing us to stop and smell the roses."

– Elizabeth Pierson

Blister Beetle

FIRST PLACE, Beetles

Blister Beetles came to the light on the front porch where
I was staying. In the mornings, they were everywhere.
This one was crawling around on some Leather Stem plants.

Canon 1V with Canon 180mm macro lens,
1/250 sec @ f/16, Fuji Sensia 100

Vermilion Flycatchers

SECOND PLACE, Flycatchers & Kingbirds

A pair of Vermilion Flycatchers made a nest and had four babies. They raised all four of them and stayed around the nest for several weeks. The family landed on this limb regularly.

Canon 1V with Canon 500mm lens and 1.4x teleconverter, 1/125 sec @ f/13, Fuji Sensia 100

Pale-winged Gray

SECOND PLACE, Camouflage/Mimicry

This moth blended in very well with the log it landed on. Sometimes the moths seemed to completely disappear and I would have to look very hard to find them.

Canon 1V with Canon 180mm f/3.5 macro lens, 1/250 sec @ f/16, Fuji Sensia

Honey Bees

FIRST PLACE, Bees, Wasps, Ants &
Other Social Insects

In the spring, swarming Honey Bees landed on the house where I was staying. The nights were still cool and the bees were not very active. They allowed me to get quite close.

Canon 1V with Canon 180mm macro lens, 1/250 sec @ f/16, Fuji Sensia 100

Red Velvet Mites

SECOND PLACE, All Other Arachnids

Red Velvet Mites would dig small holes on the wet sand and then cover up. Sometimes thousands of them could be seen.

Canon 1V with Canon 180mm macro lens 1/250 sec @ f/16, Fuji Sensia 100

Coyote

THIRD PLACE, Coyotes & Foxes

Sitting around the water hole, one never knew what would show up. I spent many hours in the blind hoping something would come. This Coyote became a regular visitor.

Canon 1V with Canon 500mm IS lens and 1.4x teleconverter, 1/125 sec @ f/13, Fuji Sensia 100

Brown-headed Cowbird

THIRD PLACE, All Other Birds

I had a bird feeder set up near the house where I was staying. Cowbirds were regular visitors but didn't always land in the right spot. This one landed on some blooming Blackbrush and stayed there just long enough.

Canon 1V with Canon 500mm f/4 IS lens and 2x teleconverter, 1/125 sec @ f/11, Fuji Sensia 100

Gulf Fritillary
THIRD PLACE, Butterflies II (Non-Skippers)

These two butterflies came flying by one day when I was trying to photograph skippers. They were coupled up and I knew they would land. I followed them for over 100 yards and, lucky for me, they did land in a good place to photograph.

Canon 1V with Canon 180mm macro lens, 1/250 @ f/16, Fuji Sensia 100

Yellow Mud Turtle
THIRD PLACE, Turtles & Tortoises

This Yellow Mud Turtle had a favorite spot on a log in the water where I was doing most of my photography. Dragonflies would land on him often, but he did not allow them to sit on his nose very long.

Canon EOS 3 with Canon 400mm f/2.8 lens and 2x teleconverter, 1/200 sec @ f/8, Fuji Sensia 100

Vermilion Flycatchers

SECOND PLACE, Animal Babies

This male Vermilion Flycatcher took very good care of his young, staying busy to keep them fed. I watched them for several weeks. One day they disappeared and I never saw them again.

Canon 1V with Canon 500mm f/4 IS lens and 2x teleconverter, 1/125 sec @ f/11, Fuji Sensia 100

Wild Turkey

THIRD PLACE, Patterns

There were many Wild Turkeys near the water hole where I was sitting. At first they were very skittish, but they got used to me being there every day and soon allowed me to get quite close.

Canon 1V with Canon 180mm f/3.5 macro lens, 1/250 sec @ f/8, Fuji Sensia 100

South Texas Shootout

PORTFOLIOS

Couch's Spadefoot Toad

FIRST PLACE, Frogs & Toads
FIRST PLACE, Reptiles & Amphibians Division

I caught this rascal one rainy night while driving the ranch roads. - D.H.

Derrick Hamrick & Roberta E. Summers, Photographers / A. Cantú Farms, Landowner

Canon EOS 3 with Canon 90mm tilt/shift lens and extension tube, 1/200 sec @ f/22, Fuji Sensia 100

Eastern Cottontail Rabbit

THIRD PLACE, Rabbits & Hares

Shooting from a blind located in a large pool, I lay in ten inches of water and put the lens one-half inch above the water line. - D.H.

Canon EOS 3 with Canon 400mm f/2.8 IS lens and 1.4x teleconverter, 1/250 sec @ f/2.8, Fuji Sensia 100

Mexican Ground Squirrel

THIRD PLACE, Rodents

I enjoyed working with this squirrel. Sometimes it would come and drink non-stop for what seemed like forever. - D.H.

Canon EOS 3 with Canon 400mm f/2.8 IS lens and 1.4x teleconverter, 1/500 sec @ f/4, Fuji Sensia 100

Mexican Ground Squirrel

SECOND PLACE, Rodents

I shot from my pool in the afternoon, lying in the steaming water for about four hours. The water was hotter than my shower back home, although the squirrel did not seem to mind. - D.H.

Canon EOS 3 with Canon 400mm 2.8 IS lens and 1.4x teleconverter, 1/1000 sec @ f/4, Fuji Sensia 100

Crayfish

SECOND PLACE, All Other Arthropods & Snails

Crayfish come out of the water and walk up muddy banks.

Canon EOS 3 with Canon 90mm tilt/shift lens and extension tube, 1/200 sec @ f/16, Fuji Sensia 100

This was a huge six-foot rattler, and the front of the lens was about twelve inches away. A homemade plexiglass shield kept me alive. The snake never struck at me. By using the tilt feature of my lens, I was able to render a sharp front-to-back image of its scales. - D.H.

Canon EOS 3 with Canon 90mm tilt/shift lens and extension tube, 1/2sec @ f/22, Fuji Sensia 100

Western Diamondback Rattlesnake

FIRST PLACE, Venomous Snakes
THIRD PLACE, Reptiles & Amphibians Division

Couch's Spadefoot Toad

FIRST PLACE, Humor
SECOND PLACE, Special Categories Division

When the toad was digging out of the mud, and opened its eye, I fired. - D.H.

Canon EOS 3 with Canon 90mm tilt/shift lens and extension tube, 1/200 sec @ f/11, Fuji Sensia 100

Ladder-backed Woodpecker

SECOND PLACE, Buntings, Grosbeaks & Woodpeckers

I only saw this woodpecker at my pool once. When it bent down to take a drink, I took the shot. I normally only got one shot with most birds. The camera's noise travels well when only one-half inch off the water. - D.H.

Canon EOS 3 with Canon 400mm f/2.8 IS lens and 1.4x teleconverter, 1/1000 @ f/4, Fuji Sensia 100

Varied Bunting

THIRD PLACE, Buntings, Grosbeaks & Woodpeckers

This Varied Bunting would come to my pool almost every aftenoon. The bird seemed to enjoy my company and sang me a tune. - D.H.

Canon EOS 3 with Canon 400mm f/2.8 IS lens and 1.4x teleconverter, 1/1000 sec @ f/4, Fuji 100 Sensia

Coyote

FIRST PLACE, Coyotes & Foxes
FIRST PLACE, Mammals Division

I hand-dug an enormous pit with a shovel, put a one-foot-high roof over it and covered it with dirt. Shooting from ground level, I took this picture a few days later during the afternoon. - D.H.

Canon Elan 7E with Canon 400mm f/2.8 IS lens and 2x teleconverter, 1/500 sec @ f/56, Fuji Sensia 100

For the longest time no roadrunners would come to my pool. But once two found it, they frequented it. They were a challenge to photograph drinking, especially with my lens almost on the water's surface. - D.H.

Canon EOS 3 with Canon 400mm f/2.8 IS lens and 1.4x teleconverter, 1/250 sec @ f/4, Fuji Sensia 100

Greater Roadrunner
FIRST PLACE, Cuckoos, Anis & Roadrunners

White-tailed Deer

FIRST PLACE, Deer
SECOND PLACE, Mammals Division

Two years ago I couldn't find a mammal on the ranch during the contest. This time I had a number of deer, Coyotes and Javelinas visiting daily. I was hoping these deer would interact when they started drinking together and was really pleased when they posed for this shot.

Dave Welling, Photographer / Pérez Ranch, Landowner

Nikon F5 with Nikon 500mm f/4-AF-S, Fuji Velvia pushed one stop

Cooper's Hawk

THIRD PLACE, Hawks & Falcons

Just as I settled into my blind at sunrise, this young Cooper's Hawk came
into the pond area to bathe. When the hawk finished bathing,
he hopped up onto this dead snag to shake off and call.

Nikon F5 with Nikon 500mm f/4 AF-S lens and 1.4x teleconverter, Fuji Velvia pushed one stop

Green-tailed Towhee

THIRD PLACE, Sparrows & Towhees

This is the first year I was able to capture good images of Green-tailed Towhees.
This little guy cooperated very well over several days, often landing
exactly where I hoped he would.

*Nikon F5 with Nikon 500mm f/4 AF-S lens and 2x teleconverter and SB-28 fill flash,
Velvia pushed one stop.*

Eastern Screech-Owl

THIRD PLACE, Camouflage / Mimicry

I believe this little guy, that I nicknamed "Otis," is the same owl I photographed two years ago. He is still "hanging out" in the same dead snag. This year it was easier to find him because I knew where to look, but he was still a challenge to see.

Nikon F-5 with Nikon 500mm f/4 AF-S lens, Velvia pushed one stop

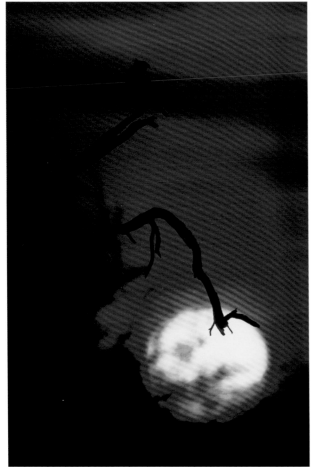

Crested Caracara

THIRD PLACE, Sunrise / Sunset

For four clear sunset days in early March, a pair of Crested Caracaras would perch on this dead mesquite snag just before sunset. They nested in May about 300 yards from this snag.

Nikon F5 with Canon Nikon 500mm f/4 AF-S lens & 1.4x teleconverter, Velvia pushed one stop

This branch, on a tree about 20 feet from my blind, was a favorite spot for a wide range of birds (I tallied over 60 species perching here at one time or another during the contest). This thrasher arrived one morning right after sunrise, and a little breeze flared its feathers just as I pushed the shutter.

Nikon F5 with Nikon 500mm f/4-AF-S lens and TC-4E 1.4x teleconverter, Velvia pushed one stop

Long-billed Thrasher
FIRST PLACE, Mockingbirds, Thrashers, Catbirds & Thrushes
FIRST PLACE, Birds Division

Harris's Hawk

FIRST PLACE, Hawks & Falcons

Of the two Harris's Hawks that came in to bathe one afternoon, this one almost got too close to photograph. This was the smaller of the two, so probably the male. He began calling to his mate as I started to photograph him.

Nikon F5 with Nikon 500mm f/4-AF-S lens, Fuji Velvia pushed one stop

Southwestern Rat Snake
(formerly Great Plains Rat Snake)
FIRST PLACE, Non-venomous Snakes II

Driving around the ranch, I noticed this small rat snake on a Christmas Cactus near the road. The weather was cool but sunny, and the snake stayed put long enough to shoot two rolls of film. - G.K.

Gary Kramer & Richard Day, Photographers
El Negro Ranch, Landowner

Canon EOS-1V, Canon 300mm f2.8 IS, 1/250sec @ f/8, Fuji Provia 100F

Little Blue Heron

FIRST PLACE, Wading Birds

This Little Blue Heron appeared only one day on our ranch. Luckily it flew directly to the log in front of me and started preening. — R.D.

Canon EOS 1V with Canon 300mm f/2.8 lens, 1/500 sec @ f/5.6, Kodak E100VSLittle

Gulf Coast Ribbon Snake

THIRD PLACE, Non-venomous Snakes I

While photographing birds from a blind next to one of the ranch ponds, I noticed a ribbon snake moving along the edge. When the snake was right in front of the blind, I stepped out and took several frames of the startled snake before it swam away. - G.K.

Canon EOS-1V with Canon 300mm f/2.8 IS lens, 1/250sec @ f/8, Fuji Velvia pushed to 100

Great Kiskadee

THIRD PLACE, Flycatchers & Kingbirds

A pair of Kiskadees frequently drank and fed near our water. One morning he sat in the early sun scouting for bugs. – R.D.

Canon EOS 1V with Canon 600mm f/4 IS lens, 1/640 sec@ f/6.3, Kodak E100VS

Black-tailed Jackrabbit

SECOND PLACE, Rabbits & Hares

This rabbit had been appearing for a few days but was very shy and wouldn't approach the water hole. Finally one morning he peeked over the mound before drinking. – R.D.

Canon ES 1V with Canon 600mm f/4 IS lens, 1/250 sec @ f/5.6, Kodak E100VS

Bobcat

SECOND PLACE, Wild Cats

During the contest, I tried a predator call on several occasions without success. Toward the end of the contest, I gave it one last try and, to my amazement, called in this Bobcat. - G.K.

Canon EOS 1V with Canon 600mm f/4 IS lens and 1.4x teleconverter, 1/500sec @ f/5.6, Fuji Provia 100F

Mediterranean Gecko

SECOND PLACE, All Other Reptiles

Alien Mediterranean Geckos apparently reached Texas shores aboard ships. They are common around human habitation. This handsome little lizard was out on a nocturnal foray, exploring a palm frond in search of insects.

John & Gloria Tveten, Photographers
Inn at Chachalaca Bend, Landowner

Minolta X-370S with Minolta 100mm macro lens and Sunpack ringlight, 1/60 sec @ f/11, Fuji Velvia

Moonseed Moth

THIRD PLACE, Moths

The large family of noctuid moths contains nearly 3,000 species that occur in North America. Few, however, are more brilliantly marked than this little Moonseed Moth, perched here on a Common Sunflower.

Minolta X-700 with Minolta 50mm macro lens, 1/60 sec @ f/16, Sunpack ringlight, Fuji Velvia

Turk's-cap White-Skipper

SECOND PLACE, Butterflies I (Skippers)

A pretty Turk's-cap White-skipper perched atop the flower of a Mexican Olive, or Anacahuite, which is widely distributed in the Rio Grande Valley. A tropical butterfly that ranges southward to Argentina, the Turk's-cap White-skipper occurs in the U.S. only in deep South Texas.

Minolta X-700 with Minolta 50mm macro lens and Sunpack ringlight, 1/60 sec @ f/22, Fuji Velvia

Leaf Beetle

SECOND PLACE, Beetles

This tiny Leaf Beetle was almost invisible on the Common Sunflower, and only through the magic of a macro lens did we discover its true beauty. Hundreds of species of Leaf Beetles in the family Chrysomelidae occur in North America.

Minolta X-370S with Minolta 50mm macro lens, 1/60 @ f/22, Sunpack ringlight, Fuji Velvia

Land Snail
THIRD PLACE, All Other Arthropods & Snails

A Land Snail crawls slowly across a fallen palm frond. We thought the spiral form of the delicate shell nicely complemented the strong, ribbed pattern of the dead frond.

Minolta X-700 with Minolta 50mm macro lens and Sunpack ringlight, 1/60 sec @ f/16, Fuji Velvia

Dainty Sulphur
SECOND PLACE, Butterflies II (Non-Skippers)

A Dainty Sulphur sips nectar at a patch of Butterweed. This is the winter form of the species, with the underside of its hindwings heavily scaled with green; the summer form is paler yellow below.

Minolta X-370s with Minolta 50mm macro lens and Sunpack ringlight, 1/60 sec @ f6, Fuji Velvia

Red-tailed Hawk

SECOND PLACE, Hawks & Falcons

An easy shot! Two hawks hung around the feeder for easy prey. This hawk was more interested in protecting his "kill" from the other hawk than in me!

Bill Burns, Photographer
Bill Burns Ranch, Landowner

Canon EOS 3 with Canon 100-400mm IS lens, 1/250 sec @ f/11, Kodak E100VS

Belted Kingfisher

SECOND PLACE, All Other Birds

I was playing a harmonica. The bird was curious. Then he "unloaded" and left. I guess he didn't like my music!

Canon EOS 3 with Canon 500mm f/4 IS lens, 1/400 sec @ f/5.6, Kodak E100VS

Northern Bobwhites

SECOND PLACE, Turkeys, Quail & Chachalacas

More luck than skill.

Canon EOS 3 with Canon 100-400mm IS lens and
1.4x teleconverter, 1/250 sec @ f/8, Kodak E100VS

Southwestern Rat Snake
(formerly Great Plains Rat Snake)
SECOND PLACE, Non-venomous Snakes II

I wanted the grasshopper, but the snake beat me to it.

Canon EOS 3 with Canon 100-400mm IS lens,
1/500 sec @ f/8, Kodak E100VS

Land Snail

FIRST PLACE, All Other Arthropods & Snails
THIRD PLACE, Insects & Arachnids Division

The snail started his journey from the top of the cactus at the left. To my surprise, his path took him over cactus spines. This picture was taken in June after a rainstorm. - J.S.

Joseph V. Smith & Don Pederson, Photographers / Cook Ranches, Landowner

Nikon N90s with Nikon 200mm f/4 micro lens, 1/250 sec @ f/11, Kodak E100VS

Pere David's Deer

THIRD PLACE, All Other Mammals

I sat in my SUV one hot June afternoon for about thirty minutes until the animal turned his head so I could capture just the right antler-head pose with the sun reflected in the animal's eye. - J.S.

Nikon N90s with Nikon 500mm f/4 P lens and 1.4x teleconverter, 1/500 sec @ f/5.6, 1/500sec, Kodak E100VS

Red Velvet Mite

FIRST PLACE, All other Arachnids

These came out in fairly large numbers the day after a hard rain and disappeared again one or two days later.

Canon A-1 with Canon 50mm macro lens and 86mm extension tube, 1/60 sec @ f/32, Fuji Provia 100F

I had taken so many shots of turtles that I told myself I would not take another one. Then these two Yellow Mud Turtles got on this log in late evening light and there went another roll of film.

Glenn Hayes, Photographer / Tecomate Ranch, Landowner

Canon EOS 3 with Canon 400mm f/2.8 lens and 2x teleconverter, 1/200 sec @ f/8, Fuji Sensia 100

Yellow Mud Turtles

FIRST PLACE, Turtles & Tortoises

Texas Toad

THIRD PLACE, Frogs & Toads

After a spring rain, toads gathered in a water hole and called to their mates. The sound of hundreds of frogs singing at the same time is unbelievably loud. A few weeks later there were thousands of tiny baby toads around the pond.

Canon EOS 3 with Canon 400mm f/2.8 lens and 540 EZ flash, 1/200 sec @ f/5.6, Fuji Sensia 100

This lizard would come to one of my morning blinds quite often. He would catch bugs and then hop up on this log and eat them. He had just finished eating a beetle when he gave me this pose.

Canon EOS 3 with Canon 400mm f/2.8 lens and 2x teleconverter, 1/200 sec @ f/8, Fuji Sensia 100

Blue Spiny Lizard
FIRST PLACE, Lizards, Skinks, Anoles & Geckos

Turkey Vultures

FIRST PLACE, Sunrise / Sunset

Sunsets on the southern plains of Texas are spectacular. From their gallery, the vultures were able to enjoy this one to the fullest.

Kermit Denver Laird, Photographer
Speer Ranch, Landowner

Nikon F5 with Nikkor 600mm f/4 AF-S lens,
1/250 sec @ f/5.6, Kodak E100VS

Burrowing Wolf-Spider

FIRST PLACE, Spiders
SECOND PLACE, Insects & Arachnids Division

Wolf-spiders go on the prowl at night. Upon locating prey, they run after it, overtake it if possible, and kill and devour it on the spot. They are willing models while dining.

Nikon F5 with Nikkor 200mm micro lens and Kenko MC7 2x teleconverter, 1/250 sec @ f/16, Kodak E100VS

Pale Wind Scorpion

THIRD PLACE, All Other Arachnids

Can you imagine this thing being the size of a dinosaur? We'd all be in trouble! Wind Scorpions are swift-running little critters that lie up during the day and forage at night on practically anything smaller and less fierce than themselves.

Nikon F5 with Nikkor 200mm micro lens and Kenko MC7 2x teleconverter, 1/250 sec @ f/16, Kodak E100VS

Eastern Screech-Owl

THIRD PLACE, Owls, Vultures & Caracaras

Roosting in a hollow dead tree about six feet high, the owl was curious and would emerge from the cavity to check out any new mice or critters. It was quite tame and we photographed it on several occasions.

Laura Elaine Moore & Steve Bensten, Photographers
McAllen Properties, Landowner

Canon EOS 1V with 500mm f/4 IS lens, 1.4x teleconverter & fill flash, Kodak E100VS

Familiar Bluet

SECOND PLACE, Dragonflies & Damselflies

This green plant was growing in a stock tank and the damselflies were landing on it. I shot from sand bags placed on the edge of the tank. – S.B.

Canon EOS 1V with Canon 100-400mm IS lens with close-up filter, f/16 & off-camera flash, Kodak E100VS

Western Coachwhip

THIRD PLACE, Non-venomous Snakes II

This was the first image I shot in the contest. I no sooner arrived at the ranch and walked around the house than I saw the snake. I retrieved my camera and voila!—my first image.

Bill Carter, Photographer
CM Cozad Ranch, Landowner

Nikon F4 with Nikon 800mm and 1.4x teleconverter, 1/250 sec @ f/8, Fuji Velvia pushed one stop

Mourning Dove

SECOND PLACE, Doves & Red-billed Pigeons

This Mourning Dove fledgling spent the better part of a day in the yard accompanied by its parent. As the sun rose in the sky, they retreated to the shade of a picnic table. By then I had my shot.

Nikon F5 with Nikon 800mm lens, 1/500 sec @ f/8, Fuji Provia 100F

Greater Arid-land Katydid

FIRST PLACE, All Other Insects
FIRST PLACE, Insects & Arachnids Division
BEST OF CONTEST

This was the last subject I shot before packing up
to return home. I almost didn't shoot it because
I had to unpack some gear to do so.

Nikon F5 with Nikon 200mm f/4 micro lens, 1/250 sec @ f/8, Fuji Velvia

Bobcat
FIRST PLACE, Wild Cats

It was just a few minutes before sunset. Without warning, the cat stepped silently out of the brush. He was very close and looked right at me. I shot two frames. Turning, he stepped casually back into the brush. The entire encounter lasted less than 90 seconds.

Hugh Lieck, Photographer
H. Yturria Ranch, Landowner

Canon EOS 3 with Canon 600mm f/4 IS lens, Fuji Velvia

Nine-banded Armadillo

THIRD PLACE, Armadillos & Mustelids

"La Chata" was practically crawling with armadillos. There were
occasions when I could see four or five at a time.
I shot quite a few photos of them, but liked this one best.

Canon EOS 3 and Canon 600mm f/4 IS lens, Fuji Velvia

Nilgai

SECOND PLACE, All other Mammals

Everybody loves the photos of the males: a White-tailed buck with huge antlers,
a jet black Nilgai bull with straight evil-looking horns. This young Nilgai cow
looked so soft and feminine that I was compelled to submit this shot.

Canon EOS 3 with Canon 600 mm f/4 IS lens and 1.4x teleconverter, Fuji Velvia

Black-crested Titmouse

SECOND PLACE, Warblers, Vireos, Kinglets, Verdins, Titmice & Gnatcatchers

Titmice are common visitors to bird feeders in the Valley, but they are very active and often hard to photograph. I got this one to sit still long enough by hiding a water dripper behind the lichen-covered perch.

Michael Delesantro, Photographer
Skipper Ranch, Lanowner

*Canon EOS 3 with Canon 600mm f/4 IS lens and 1.4x teleconverter,
1/250 sec @ f/8, Fuji Provia 100F*

Brown-headed Cowbird

THIRD PLACE, Animal Babies

I watched a pair of Painted Buntings build and tend a nest. When I was confident that the young birds were nearly grown, I visited the nest, only to find this single cowbird chick.

*Canon A2E with Canon 180mm f/3.5 macro lens,
1/125 sec @ f/11, Fuji Sensia 100*

Orange-crowned Warbler

THIRD PLACE, Warblers, Vireos, Kinglets, Verdins, Titmice & Gnatcatchers

This Orange-crowned Warbler spent the winter at Skipper Ranch and
visited a birdbath every day. On the day this photo was taken
it was quite hot. The bird was panting to help cool itself off.

*Canon EOS 3 with 600mm f/4 IS lens and 1.4x teleconverter,
1/200 sec @ f/8 with fill flash, Fuji Provia 100F*

American Alligator

FIRST PLACE, All other Reptiles

In the predawn light I saw this 13-foot alligator amble toward the pond, stopping momentarily at the water's edge. He opened and closed his mouth numerous times. I snapped this picture when the first rays of sunlight crept into his gigantic jaws. - M.D.

Mary Jo Janovsky & Mary Donahue, Photographers / RGV Outdoors Center, Inc., Landowner

Canon EOS 3 with Canon 500mm f/4 IS lens; Fuji Provia 100F

Mediterranean Gecko

THIRD PLACE, All other Reptiles

Suspended by the suction cups on his feet, his soft skin, short stout body and large head were almost transparent and well-camouflaged against the log. What a marvel! - M.J.

Canon EOS 3 with Canon 100-400mm IS lens, Fuji Provia 100F pushed one stop

American Badger

FIRST PLACE, Armadillos & Mustelids

This Badger and I spent about one hour together one day. She allowed me to reposition my blind (my car) to get photos from several angles. This photo was taken when she was about 14 feet away and just before she fell asleep by my car. - G.Mc.

Gary & Chris McHale, Photographers / H. Yturria Ranch, Landowner

Nikon F5 with Nikon 400mm f/2.8 lens, Kodak E100VS

Bobcat

THIRD PLACE, Wild Cats

I was amazed one day when this Bobcat gave me
a great opportunity to photograph her. Although
I was taking this photo from my car, she walked right up
within 25 feet and sat there for about five minutes. - G.Mc.

Gary & Chris McHale, Photographer
H. Yturria Ranch, Landowner

Nikon F5 with Nikon with 400mm f/2.8 lens,
1/250 sec @ f/2.8, Kodak E100VS

Common Pauraque

SECOND PLACE, Swallows, Swifts, Nightjars & Hummingbirds

Landowner Sharon Waite and I found this Pauraque in an orange orchard. She pointed a spotlight at the bird and I crawled on my stomach a few feet at a time until I could shoot from six feet away.

John Pickles, Photographer
William Richard Buchholz & Waite / Metz Farm, Landowners

Canon EOS 1V with Canon 100-400mm IS lens, 1/3 sec @ f/5.6, Fuji Provia 100F

Western Diamondback Rattlesnake

SECOND PLACE, Venomous Snakes

This six-foot Western Diamondback was found lying in ambush behind the front door of the main ranch house. It was "forcibly" moved to a more photogenic location among the wildflowers and then released in a remote location.

David Powell & Donald Bartram, Photographers
Mary B. Ranch / William & Mary Bertha Mallet, Landowners

Nikon F5 with Nikon 500mm f4 ED AFS lens and extension tube, Fuji Provia 100F

I was looking for frogs, when I found myself in a Louisiana Waterthrush's feeding terrritory. The little brown bird walked right under my tripod, paying no attention to me. After several rolls of film I slipped away unnoticed while he continued his quest for bugs.

Julieanne Harris, Photographer / Skipper Ranch, Landowner

Canon 1V with Canon 500mm lens with extension tubes, Fuji Velvia pushed one stop

Louisiana Waterthrush
FIRST PLACE, Warblers, Vireos, Kinglets,
Verdins, Titmice & Gnatcatchers

Merriam's Pocket Mouse

FIRST PLACE, Rodents

This tiny mouse lived under my cabin. He would emerge from his hole, eat a few seeds, and scamper off. Several times, I lost sight of him only to find him looking at me from two inches away. I wonder what he was thinking.

Irene Hinke-Sacilotto, Photographer / H. Yturria Ranch, Landowner

Nikon F5 with Nikon 200mm micro lens, 1/80 sec @ f/4 with flash, Fuji Sensia 100

Texas Tortoise

SECOND PLACE, Turtles & Tortoises

I found this tortoise behind the bunkhouse. He lived there for six weeks and became quite friendly. Lying on my belly in the dirt, I caught this shot of him "hauling shell" back to his prickly-pear home.

Dennis Erhart, Photographer
Weaver Ranch, Landowner

Canon EOS 1N with Canon 600mm f/4 lens,
/500 @ f/5.6, Kodak E100VS

Texas Toad

SECOND PLACE, Frogs & Toads

Preparation, patience and persistence were major requirements for this shot. High-speed flash and a Phototrap were used to capture this Texas Toad in mid-jump.

Linda F. Peterson, Photographer
Joe E. Chapa Family Ranch, Landowner

Canon EOS 1N-RS, 180mm macro lens,
1/200 sec @ f/18, Kodak E100VS

Groove-billed Ani

THIRD PLACE, Cuckoos, Anis & Roadrunners

Groove-billed Anis are black grackle-sized birds with a large, heavy curved bill. They keep to thick brushy areas.

Pedro Garcia, Photographer
Guerra Brothers Ranch, Landowner

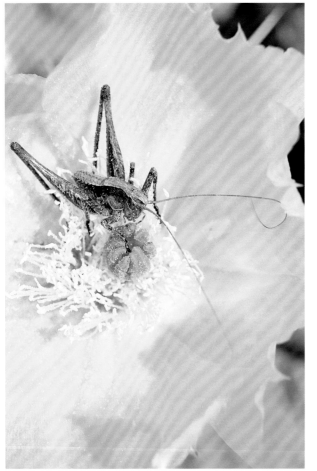

Decticine Katydid

THIRD PLACE, All Other Insects

Searching for "the small" on a gray windy day, I discovered a grasshopper, battling to hold on to his position in a Prickly Pear bloom. The wind abated just long enough to capture this shot. - L.B.W.

Lynn Bieber-Weir & Ray Bieber, Photographers
El Devisadero Ranch, M & A Garcia, Landowners

Canon EOS 3 with Tamron 90mm macro lens, Fuji Provia 100F pushed one stop

The day before, I spooked these Nilgai before I saw them. The next day, I waited under a tree in full camouflage and got lucky. I got only eight frames and this was the only one with all three muzzles in the water. – J.B.

Jim & Deva Burns, Photographers / Monica & Ray Burdette, Landowners

Canon EOS 1V with Canon 400mm f/2.8 lens and 2x teleconverter, 1/60 sec @ f/8, Fuji Velvia

Nilgai
FIRST PLACE, All other Mammals

Nine-banded Armadillo

SECOND PLACE, Armadillos & Mustelids

This armadillo was a regular visitor to my watering hole. I was sitting in my blind at dusk, just waiting for the light to become perfect, and he came in for his regular evening drink. — M.W.

Mark & Sue Werner, Photographers
McAllen Properties, Landowner

EOS 3 with Canon 100-400mm IS lens, Fuji Velvia set to ISO 40

Black-bellied Whistling-Ducks

THIRD PLACE, Rails, Gallinules, Coots, Grebes, Ducks & Geese

At the edge of a resaca, I waited a couple of hours for the ducks to get closer. When I rose to leave, I pushed the tripod down into the mud further to help me out. When I finally extracted the tripod, the mud had sucked the feet right off.

Fred LaBounty, Photographer
Krenmueller Farms / Bert & Trudy Forthuber, Landowners

EOS 1V with Canon EF 500mm f/4 IS lens, Fuji Sensia 100

Southern Broken-Dash

THIRD PLACE, Butterflies I (Skippers)

These small skippers have a darting flight-and-land pattern. I could not predict where they would land. After hours of moving all over and moving the camera in and out of focus, I knew that yoga training would be my next step to improving my photo skills!

Merrill Nix, Photographer
Lockett / McManus, Landowners

Nikon F5 with Nikkor AF 60mm micro lens and SB28 fill flash, Fuji Provia 100F

White-tailed Deer

THIRD PLACE, Deer
PEOPLE'S CHOICE

A prolonged dry spell led this young buck to a small pond where we were photographing birds.

Randall Ennis & Alberto Gutierrez, Photographers
San Pedro Ranch / Baldo & Danny Vela, Landowners

Canon 1V with Canon 300mm f/2.8 lens and 2x teleconverter, Fuji Provia 100F

Rare Cat Award

The Rare Cat Award was created to focus on three rare and elusive cats of South Texas. Ocelots and Jaguarundis require dense pockets of nearly impenetrable thorn brush for their survival and Mountain Lions need large open territories where they may flourish and raise young. These cats and their habitat are severely threatened by the expansive growth taking place in South Texas. The $5,000 award for a winning photo would reward both photographer and landowner while furnishing the public an extraordinary glimpse of these marvelous creatures. There were no photos submitted in the 2002 contest.

(L-R) Jaguarundi, Mountain Lion, Ocelot

Artwork created by Esperanza S. Chapa
from original photos by
Wendy Shattil & Bob Rozinski,
dancingpelican.com

South Texas Shootout Judges

George D. Lepp
Los Osos, California
Outdoor & Nature Photographer, Lecturer & Author
Lepp & Associates

George D. Lepp has been capturing beautiful photographic images for over 25 years and shares his knowledge with other photographers through lectures, workshops and writing. He is Field Editor for *Outdoor Photographer* and *PC Photo* magazines, is Publisher and Editor of his own photography journal, *The Natural Image*, and presents a nationwide lecture series on photographic techniques.

Deborah Free
Pavilion, New York
Photographer/Stock Agency Consultant
Deborah Free - Image Consultant, L.L.C.

Deborah Free travels the world to work extensively with both the photographers and stock agencies. With over 15 years of experience in the field of photography, she is continually building on her extensive knowledge of the stock photography industry, taking that knowledge to photographers to help them and their businesses grow to the next level. She is the past President, CEO and Manager of nature stock agency Natural Selection.

Cliff Beittel
York, Pennsylvania
Professional Wildlife Photographer & Author

Cliff Beittel has been a full-time nature and wildlife photographer since 1992, specializing in birds, birdwatchers, birding hotspots and associated wildlife. His images have appeared in all the major U.S. birding magazines and in many books and calendars. As the First Grand Prize winner in The Valley Land Fund's 1998 contest, he is the first former champion to serve on the judging panel.

(L-R) George D. Lepp, Deborah Free, Cliff Beittel
Photo by Ruth Hoyt

Small Tract Competition

The Small Tract Competition is based on the South Texas Shootout but designed for landowners with fewer than 100 acres of land and photographers who want to compete but not at the Shootout's grueling level. The small tract landowner provides the photographer with access to the property, where the contest photographs are to be taken. The photographer's job is to find and photograph species from five wildlife divisions, and create a portfolio of 25 images to enter in the contest.

A panel of three judges awards points to each slide, and the highest-scoring slides compete for first, second and third places and bonus points in their respective divisions. The five division winners compete for Best of Contest and more bonus points.

At the end of judging, the landowner-photographer team with the most points is declared the grand prize winner and the first place prize money is divided between them. Prize money is awarded through 25th place. The People's Choice award is determined by popular vote at the El Monte awards event.

–Ruth Hoyt

BEST OF CONTEST
Photographer: Patty Raney / Landowner: CL & Patty Raney

Small Tract Competition

First Grand Prize

Rex Hewitt, Photographer
J.D. Hensz, Landowner
Rio Viejo, Bayview

Photographer Rex Hewitt and landowner J.D. Hensz met during a fishing trip in 1997. J.D. caught a sailfish about 50 miles off shore, but didn't have a camera on board to document the event. He got on the radio and called out for anyone with a camera. Rex responded and cruised on by to capture the moment on film. Since then the two have participated as a team in two of The Valley Land Fund wildlife photo contests.

Rex compares his experience in the 2002 wildlife photo contest with a scene from a classic movie. "In *The Wizard of Oz*, when Dorothy lands in Oz and all the little munchkins run away, that's kind of like being in the brush. When you walk into the brush, all the little animals are going to run and hide. And then you've just got to sit and wait for them to all come out again. You'd be surprised at all the little things that come out."

He worked at J.D.'s twelve-and-a-half-acre property near Bayview in Cameron County. J.D. has left most of the area to mother nature except for a small niche carved out for his house. "It's low maintenance on the lawn work," he says. The landscape is primarily brushy, native habitat with a resaca that curves around it on three sides. His two-story house has made for the perfect viewing blind.

From the second floor he has watched a bobcat meander along his driveway, and has witnessed nine-foot alligators visiting the resaca out back.

J.D. has documented about 300 species on his small property since first participating in the contest. "Acre for acre, I've got as many species as anybody else, if not more." Rex can attest to the wide variety, "On the last day I saw two birds–one a Mockingbird. They were looking down, and I wondered, 'What are they looking at?' Then I saw a six-foot Indigo snake; they were jumping on him."

Rex was more welcome on his visits to the property than the Indigo. "There was an oriole that would follow me in. When I'd come to the gate, he'd follow me, because I'd put oranges out every day. And he was waiting for me to come out here."

Run-ins with ticks and cactus needles during the past two competitions almost kept Rex from signing on again in 2002. But J.D. managed to talk him into it. And obviously it was a good thing he did. J.D. asks ironically, "Could we have done any better?"

–Eryn Reddell Wingert

Immature Leaf-footed Bug

FIRST PLACE, Insects & Arachnids

I was searching for something to photograph around a group of cacti when I noticed an ant carrying a butterfly wing. When I got down for a closer look, I discovered green bugs the same color as the cactus.

Canon 1V with Canon 100mm f/2.8 macro lens, 1/60 sec @ f/22, Fuji Velvia

Texas Spiny Lizard

SECOND PLACE, Reptiles & Amphibians

I never knew when I would find something to photograph. This lizard was sleeping between two cactus pads. I did not notice the tiny red bug above the lizard until I saw the developed slides.

Canon 1V with Canon 100mm f/2.8 macro lens, 1/125 sec @ f/16, Fuji Velvia

Orbweaver Spider

THIRD PLACE, Spiders

On the last day of the contest, I went to an area of the property that I had not visited before. I made my way through some thick brush and found this unusual spider working on his web in a thorn bush.

Canon 1V with Canon 100mm f2.8 macro lens, 1/60 sec @ f/22, Velvia

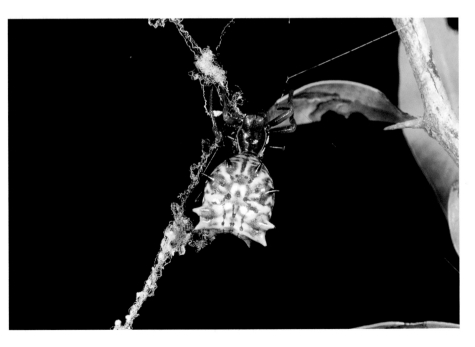

Willet

SECOND PLACE, Birds

As I approached the resaca, a bird came toward me
in a defensive manner. Perhaps he was guarding a nesting area,
but I did not see a nest. He calmed down a bit, and I was able
to shoot a few frames before leaving the bird's territory.

Canon 1V with Canon 600mm f/4 IS lens, 1/125 sec @ f/16, Velvia

Eastern Cottontail

THIRD PLACE, Mammals

I really enjoy photographing rabbits. After watching the rabbits for a few days, I noticed a variety of personalities. This one seems to be saying a prayer before starting his day.

Canon 1V with 600mm f/4 IS lens, 1/60 sec @ f/9, Fuji Velvia

Second Grand Prize

Victor E. Sanchez, Photographer
Marsha Gamel Nelson, Landowner
El Rocio, Mission

El Rocio Retreat Center is a wooded 18-acre property in Mission, Texas that Marsha Gamel Nelson has nurtured for the past nine years. About a mile from the Rio Grande River, it is a meeting and party venue, a bed and breakfast, and a retreat center. It is also home to Raccoons, Green Jays, Greater Roadrunners, Chachalacas and Beavers, among other South Texas wildlife.

The property has competed in all of the VLF wildlife photo contests since the beginning, and photographers have produced some truly memorable photos there. Marsha especially likes the Small Tract Competition because it reinforces the message that small tracts are vital to the survival of the Valley's native plants and animals.

During the 2002 photo contest, high school band director Victor E. Sanchez could be found most late afternoons draped in camouflage, prowling the grounds of El Rocio. This was his first time in the photo contest and his most memorable experience was watching a large Texas Indigo Snake climb a palm tree and chase out a screech owl and some field mice in its search for dinner.

Photography became Victor's hobby three years ago when he decided to document with his camera some of the wildlife he was seeing. He is eagerly looking forward to the next competition.

Marsha says the contest supports her belief that, because the Valley is changing so rapidly, there is a very real need to preserve what we can now. She believes "it gives like-minded people the opportunity to come together for the appreciation and preservation of nature."

– Audrey G. Martin

I was lying on the ground near the pond looking for the local water snake when I was startled by a noise. As I turned to investigate, I noticed a male ground squirrel, on the right, playfully approaching a female in heat.

Canon Elan IIe with Canon 75-300mm IS lens, 1/250 sec @ f/5.6, Fuji Sensia 100

Mexican Ground Squirrels

FIRST PLACE, Mammals

Forked-tailed Bush Katydid

FIRST PLACE, Special Categories

This katydid was basking in the sun just before sundown near the property's edge. By making a slight adjustment to the grass stem, I was able to position the insect right where I wanted it.

Canon EOS 3 with Canon 75-300mm IS lens,
1/1000 sec @ f/4, Fuji Velvia

Mexican Ground Squirrel

SECOND PLACE, Mammals

I watched ground squirrels drink from the pond for several days. I slowly made them aware of me and moved closer to them. Within a week I was able to get on the ground for this shot.

Canon EOS 3 with Canon 500mm f/4.0 IS lens, 1/125 sec @ f/5.6, Fuji Velvia

Great Kiskadee

THIRD PLACE, Birds

The early-morning call of this Great Kiskadee led me straight to him. He was hopping from tree to tree near my feeder.

Canon Elan IIe with Canon 500mm IS lens, 1/125 @ f/11, Fuji Sensia 100

Western Ribbon Snake

FIRST PLACE, Reptiles & Amphibians

While looking for insects on the plant life near the pond,
I noticed this snake moving toward the wooden dock.
I moved quickly, got down on my stomach, and
rested the camera on the dock floor.

*Canon EOS 3 with Sigma 400mm APO lens and extension tube,
1/60 sec @ f/5.6, Fuji Sensia 100*

Third Grand Prize

Scarlet & George Colley, Photographers
Barbara Kennett, Landowner
South Padre Island

Seven years ago, Barbara Kennett had all the lawn torn from her 50-foot-by-100-foot lot on which her house stood. It was shortly after a nature festival in Harlingen when she realized that her imported landscape was not enough to welcome droves of wildlife.

Now, native plants surround her home on South Padre Island, and the birds and photographers are having a heyday. "The birds need cover, food and water, which is what I've tried to provide for them," Barbara says. "In return, I have lots of company."

Scarlet Colley was among the visitors who discovered worlds in Barbara's tiny lot brimming with wildlife. She had spent five years visiting Barbara, learning about birds and helping her care for her lush yard that includes three waterfalls and two streams that recycle the water.

But when Scarlet entered the 2002 Small Tract Competition, having a simple camera and barely any still-photography experience, the lot took on a new meaning. Suddenly, she knew the yard, just four blocks from her own, in a different way.

"I had been going to Barbara's for years, but when it came to the contest, all of a sudden I became much more intimate with the yard," Scarlet said. "I had never really seen her yard in the same way."

Because she didn't have many lenses from which to choose, Scarlet concentrated on the tiniest critters in the yard while other photographers scoured the yard snapping photos of birds.

The photo of a Green Anole Lizard shedding its skin was among Scarlet's favorites. She's also proud of the up-close photo of a caterpillar she caught on a dreary day when most of the yard was quiet and inactive. It was the only creature she saw that day.

Scarlet plans to forego the 2004 contest to concentrate on what she says is her true passion, dolphins, which she's been filming for eight years. She is an advisory board member for The Valley Land Fund and plans to stay involved in conservation.

–Elizabeth Pierson

Green Anole

THIRD PLACE, Reptiles & Amphibians

We had photographed all morning at the back pond.
Just as we stepped out the front door for lunch
I spotted this shrouded anole. Lunch had to wait.
He was actually eating his molting skin.

Canon EOS A2 with Canon 100mm macro lens, Fuji Sensia 100

Caterpillar

THIRD PLACE, Special Categories

This caterpillar was the only creature I could find to film
that day. I found it on landowner Barbara Kennett's
Blue Mistflowers outside her back door, protected from the
wind. Its beautiful pattern drew me to work close-in.

Canon EOS A2 with Canon 100mm macro lens, Sensia 100

Fourth Grand Prize

Bryan & Linh Thiel, Photographers
Charles & Lana Vieh, Landowners
Vieh's Bed & Breakfast, San Benito

When Bryan and Linh Thiel of Houston entered the 2002 Small Tract Competition, they admit that they didn't know the difference between a titmouse and a field mouse. "We were really pleasantly surprised going into it. With it being our first contest, we didn't have any expectations, and we thought of it more as a learning experience," says Bryan.

The Thiels paired with Lana and Charles Vieh, the owners of Vieh's Bed & Breakfast, south of San Benito. This was the Viehs' fourth wildlife photo contest. "It's fun. You learn a lot from the photographers. They're really patient about showing you different things," Lana says. "How much I retain, that's another thing." Charles agrees and adds," Those pictures don't just happen."

Their love of the outdoors led Bryan and Linh to take up photography. They learned about the contest while surfing the Internet and decided to try it out. They would drive down from Houston on weekends. "It was nice," says Bryan. "It was a long drive, but it gave us time to unwind and visit with one another."

Charles and Lana warmly welcomed them into their home, setting them up in one of their cozy rooms. Their hospitality did not stop there. "Lana would leave Benadryl by our bedside for Lihn. I don't have to wear bug repellent if I take my wife outside. It doesn't matter how much repellent she puts on; it's like barbecue sauce for the bugs," shares Bryan.

"Mi Casa es Su Casa" is the slogan for the bed and breakfast and is not limited to people. Over 120 species of birds have been spotted on the fifteen-plus acre property. The Black-bellied Whistling-Duck claims the title of mascot. It was not hard for Bryan and Linh to figure out why the birds felt so welcome. During their visits, Charles worked on building all kinds of little houses for the visiting fowl.

Despite losing a 600mm lens to water damage and the bugs that Linh battled, the Thiels are continuing their educational journey with photography. And the Viehs plan to continue welcoming visitors to their little paradise.

–Eryn Reddell Wingert

Black-crowned Night-Heron

HONORABLE MENTION, Birds

We came in late Friday night, and I set up camp out next to the pond. The next morning I awoke to birds chirping and saw this Night-Heron on the shoreline next to my camp. - B.T.

Nikon F100 with 600mm Nikon AF-S lens, Fuji 100 Sensia II

Common Pauraque

HONORABLE MENTION, Special Categories

I was walking and saw this bird fly like a butterfly. I walked to where she was sitting and saw two eggs on the ground. - B.T.

Nikon F100 with Nikon 80-400mm VR lens, Fuji Sensia II 100

Fifth Grand Prize

Patty Raney, Photographer
C.L. & Patty Raney, Landowners
Harlingen

Tucked away in the back corner of a mobile home park, not far from Valle Vista Mall in Harlingen, is a special little piece of habitat where Patty Raney snapped the shot that won the Best of Contest and People's Choice Awards, and helped her capture Fifth Grand Prize.

These two ducks were cooling off in the front yard when Patty snapped the picture.

Some twenty years ago, her husband "Skip" traded a motorcycle for the land, and they have lived there ever since. Their two lots total less than one-half acre, yet their land lies next to a drainage canal. The area is home to every sort of bird and wild critter that can exist in this suburban setting. In contrast to their neighbors' neatly trimmed yards, the Raneys' land is more natural, with some brush piles and a portion of the canal bank's habitat left uncut.

Patty has been an avid birder for many years. But about five years ago, when Skip's camera equipment mysteriously began to disappear, he realized that his wife was taking this photography seriously. Her work is featured in the December 2002 issue of *Birder's World*.

Patty is a very focused lady, a dental hygienist who is filling her "family album" with portraits of the natural family all around her. Every week, she puts out some 100 pounds of her homemade birdseed mixture, a special blend including something for each of the different species that may arrive at the feeders.

Her neighbors smile at the lady with the "AVOCET" license plate and the 20-foot-tall, custom-made photo blind in her yard. Patty uses that height to photograph the red-crowned parrots and other birds that frequent the trees on the canal bank.

Patty and Skip are looking forward to the 2004 competition. Her advice: "Have fun with it!"

–Audrey G. Martin

Through the camera lens, my personal world disappears and I become a part of nature's. I was able to share in the fun these ducks were having in this brief but welcome shower.

Minolta Maxxum 9 with AF Reflex 500 lens, Unknown speed, Kodak Elite Chrome

Black-bellied Whistling-Ducks

FIRST PLACE, Birds
BEST OF CONTEST
PEOPLE'S CHOICE

Small Tract Competition

PORTFOLIOS

Eastern Amberwing Dragonfly

SECOND PLACE, Special Categories

Waiting for this dragonfly to light on a Bougainvillea perch, I was delighted when it lighted on this flower right next to me and gave me this shot.

Rafa Flores, Photographer
AV Shull Properties, Landowner

Canon EOS-1V with Canon 180mm macro lens, Fuji Sensia 100

Wasp Species

SECOND PLACE, Insects & Arachnids

I first noticed the small green buds of this plant in late March. By April they had turned into beautiful flowers, and I discovered many different butterflies and bees visiting them. The bee's speed and movement proved a real challenge as it buzzed from flower to flower. - E.S.C.

Esperanza S. Chapa & Daniel A. Montelongo Lugo, Photographers
El Rocio, Landowner

Canon Rebel 2000 with Canon 100-400mm IS lens, 1/125sec @ f/4.2, Fuji Sensia 100

Youth Photo Contest

The Youth Photo Contest is designed to attract young photographers, ages 14-18 years. Unlike photographers from the South Texas Shootout and Small Tract Competition, youth participants are allowed to take their contest photos anywhere in the eight counties of South Texas except at a zoo. Their job is to find and photograph species from five wildlife divisions, and create a portfolio of 25 images to enter in the contest.

A panel of three judges awards points to each slide, and the highest-scoring slides compete for first, second and third places and bonus points in their respective divisions. The five division winners compete for Best of Contest and more bonus points.

At the end of judging, the photographer with the most points is declared the grand prize winner. Not only does the winner receive a cash prize but a trip to attend the North American Nature Photography Association's annual summit as well. Prize money is awarded through 25th place. The People's Choice award is determined by popular vote at the El Monte awards event.

–Ruth Hoyt

BEST OF CONTEST
Photographer: Blaine Davis

Youth Photo Contest

PORTFOLIOS

A Family Experience

When my sons told me they wanted to compete in the first-ever Valley Land Fund Youth Photo Contest, I was thrilled. The only problem was we did not own a proper still camera. Actually, they had been using a small digital camera for a couple of years, but that was not an option.

Buying a quality 35mm camera with an adequate lens was also not in our budget, but my wife Linda and I decided that if they really wanted to enter, we would make it happen.

We sought advice, shopped around and settled on a Canon EOS-3 with a small telephoto lens. Taplin, 17, and Schuyler, 15, understood that they would be sharing this new acquisition.

Just like all the other youngsters entered in the contest, my boys were pretty much limited to weekends or the occasional holiday during the early months of the contest. However, when school ended for the summer and many contestants would be shooting daily, my guys had a prior commitment. They were headed to Europe.

So, we got up early nearly every weekend and stayed out late on many a weekday chasing the photographers' rich light of early morning and late afternoon. Oh sure, we faced the occasional reluctance to arise and the inevitable acrimony of sibling sharing, but we got through it.

Wildlife photography is a very challenging endeavor, even for the most patient of adults. Most people, young or old, are simply not interested in spending hours in a sweltering South Texas photo blind, Taplin and Schuyler included. However, they set up scaffolding, assembled blinds, arranged perches, held reflectors for one another, and occasionally even agreed on whose turn it was to take pictures.

Spending time in the outdoors is quality time, and when you combine that with spending time with your children, that's a double bonus. Photographing wildlife also teaches unique life lessons. It requires a person to pause from the frenetic pace of everyday life and appreciate the natural world.

The Valley Land Fund Youth Photo Contest was one of the greatest experiences my family has ever shared. There are so many wonderful memories of time well spent.

I will never forget the excitement in Taplin's voice when he ran back to camp for more film because he was "getting the best shots of a horny toad that I've ever gotten." Or Schuyler, when he pedaled back home from his scaffold blind on the parrots in our neighborhood and blurted out, "I've shot three rolls of film, and the parrots are still there if Taplin wants to try!"

Thank you, Valley Land Fund, for a great contest! And thank you, Taplin and Schuyler, for all the wonderful memories we will share for a lifetime. And whose turn is it to use the camera, anyway?

–Richard Moore

First Grand Prize
Richard Taplin Moore

Tarantula
FIRST PLACE, Insects & Arachnids

I tied each antler with yarn and hung the skull from a birdfeeder. After myriad attempts, the tarantula finally posed between the two eye cavities.

Canon EOS 3 with Canon 75-300mm lens, Provia 100F

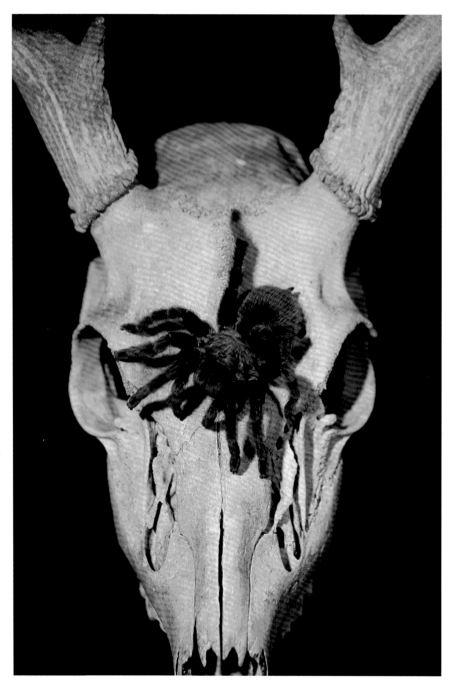

Buff-bellied Hummingbird

FIRST PLACE, Birds

I snapped this shot as the Buff-bellied Hummingbird leaned into flight. Hummingbirds are perhaps the most frenetic creatures in the wild.

Canon EOS 3 with Canon 75-300mm lens, Fuji Provia 100F

Raccoon

SECOND PLACE, Mammals

This little guy was very cooperative, even sticking his tongue out at me. Unfortunately, that shot was out of focus.

Canon EOS 3 with Canon 75-300mm lens, Provia 100F

Monarch

SECOND PLACE, Insects & Arachnids

Moments after emerging from its chrysalis, this Monarch began to pump fluid into its wings. After about half an hour, it began to prep its wings for flight.

Canon EOS 3 with Canon 75-300mm lens, Provia 100F

Texas Tortoise

THIRD PLACE, Reptiles & Amphibians

I spotted this tortoise eating near a cactus when I was
driving home from photographing Bobcats
near Rio Grande City. I quickly took a few shots,
but was certain I wouldn't enter them in the contest.

Canon EOS 3 with Canon 75-300mm lens, Fuji Provia 100F

Second Grand Prize
Blaine Davis

American Elk
FIRST PLACE, Mammals

The property adjacent to the McAllen Ranch had several exotic species that I managed to shoot through the fence. This particular one stood still for a good half roll of film.

Canon 1N with Canon 100-400mm IS lens, Fuji Sensia

Red-tailed Hawk

FIRST PLACE, Special Categories
BEST OF CONTEST

We were driving back in for the night, looking along the fenceline for a last shot or two, when we saw this hawk about 50 yards on the other side of the barbed-wire fence. We barely made it close enough before the sun went too far down to capture the shot.

Canon 1N with Canon 500mm lens with 2x teleconverter, Fuji Sensia

Western Diamondback Rattlesnake

FIRST PLACE, Reptiles & Amphibians

The blind I was waiting in was basically a small tent with no bottom except for some carpeting that covered the bottom edges of the tent. After taking a drink, the rattlesnake came straight toward the blind and disappeared. When I found it again, it was alongside the tent. At that point I could see that it was at least six feet long.

Canon 1N with Canon 100-400mm IS lens, Fuji Sensia

Southern Dogface

THIRD PLACE, Insects & Arachnids

Using a macro lens to photograph butterflies makes you notice exactly how narrow your depth of field really is, especially when it's windy.

Nikon F4 with 75-180mm micro lens, Fuji Sensia

Third Grand Prize
Schuyler Moore

Red-crowned Parrot
SECOND PLACE, Birds

Someone in our neighborhood had an old palm tree trunk with parrots roosting inside it every afternoon.

Canon EOS 3 with Canon 75-300mm lens, Provia 100F

Gulls
SECOND PLACE, Special Categories

I threw bread up in the air and captured the gulls in the sunset.

Canon EOS 3 with Canon 75-300mm lens, Fuji Provia 100F

Bobcat

THIRD PLACE, Mammals

I found this baby Bobcat and snapped pictures
of him as he explored a tree.

Canon EOS 3 with Canon 75-300mm lens, Provia 100F

Buff-bellied Hummingbird

THIRD PLACE, Birds

This hummingbird posed on a branch after it had
a quick drink from the feeder.

Canon EOS 3 with Canon 75-300mm lens, Provia 100F

Fourth Grand Prize
Analisa Rodriguez

Black Witch

HONORABLE MENTION, Insects & Arachnids

I spotted it on my front door then chased it all over my house so it could land on a tree. Finally, when I saw it on the tree outside my room, I took the picture. It was perfect!

Canon EOS Rebel 2000 with Canon 1SX 300mm lens, Fuji Sensia 100

Fifth Grand Prize
Stephen Leidner

Virginia Opossum

HONORABLE MENTION, Mammals

The nocturnal opossum spends most of its time foraging for food. I photographed this critter as he scurried through my backyard.

Pentax LX with Vivitar 135mm f/2.8 macro lens, 1/60 sec @ f/8, Fuji Sensia II 100

American Alligator

SECOND PLACE, Reptiles & Amphibians

This photograph was taken from the bed of a truck, about ten or fifteen feet from the subject. By the time I got to the alligator, it was irritable and hungry—I didn't want to be its morning snack.

Erin Keelin, Photographer

Canon AE-1 Program with Canon 75-205mm lens, S: 1/500 sec and A: Automatic, Kodak Elite 100

Laughing Gulls

THIRD PLACE, Special Categories

One morning in June, I took a drive to South Padre Island and went for a walk on the beach. I came upon a flock of gulls and I started snapping shots of them at random.

Stephanie Chavez, Photographer

Canon EOS Rebel 2000 with 28-80mm lens

Small Tract Competition and Youth Photo Contest Judges

Lance Krueger
Edinburg, Texas
Wildlife Photographer

Lance Krueger is a full-time professional photographer and outdoor writer with a BBA in Marketing from the University of Texas-Pan American. He travels extensively every fall and winter across the United States and Canada in pursuit of photos of game species. As an active member of the Outdoor Writers' Association of America and the North American Nature Photography Association, his images appear in magazines, books, calendars, brochures, advertisements and other periodicals.

Larry Ditto
McAllen, Texas
Nature Photographer

Larry Ditto has been engaged in nature photography for nearly 30 years. Until 1999 when he retired, he worked as a refuge manager in the National Wildlife Refuge System, including Santa Ana/Lower Rio Grande Valley Reserves. In 2000, he partnered with Greg Lasley of Austin to win First Grand Prize in The Valley Land Fund's South Texas Shootout. His work has has appeared in numerous publications.

Ruth Hoyt
McAllen, Texas
Nature Photographer / Photo Contest Director
The Valley Land Fund

Ruth Hoyt left St. Louis, Missouri in 2000 to become the Photo Contest Director for The Valley Land Fund. Her photography has been seen in a myriad of publications. She is a charter member of the North American Nature Photography Association and founder, Past President and Chairman of the Board for Missouri Nature and Environmental Photographers. Ruth formed a sister organization, Texas Nature and Environmental Photographers. Ruth teaches nature photography, leads workshops and is well known for her engaging multimedia slide show presentations.

Photographers: Esperanza S. Chapa & Daniel A. Montelongo Lugo
Landowner: El Rocio

Fourth Grade Nature Photo Contest

The contest is designed to teach Rio Grande Valley fourth graders to observe and learn about the natural world around them, while having fun. During March 2003 the students combed private and public land in the eight southernmost counties in Texas, seeking photographic subjects such as animals, animal homes, water and scenic views. Teachers collected the photographs and turned them in to The Valley Land Fund's office for judging. Of the 75 winning photos from the contest, the eight division winners are highlighted in the pages ahead. Of these eight, five were designated as Grand Prize winners.

– Ruth Hoyt

BEST OF CONTEST
Photographer: Avery W.C. Danielson / Palmer-Laakso Elementary School, Los Fresnos

Fourth Grade

Brazilian Free-tailed Bat

(formerly Mexican Freetail Bat)

FIRST GRAND PRIZE
FIRST PLACE, Animal Homes Division
FIRST PLACE, Animal Holes

Avery W.C. Danielson, Photographer
Mrs. Narvaez-Gonzalez, Teacher
Palmer-Laakso Elementary School, Los Fresnos

Scenic View

SECOND GRAND PRIZE
FIRST PLACE, Scenic Views Division
FIRST PLACE, Sunrises, Sunsets

Shelby W. Peters, Photographer
Mrs. Tankersly, Teacher
Saint John's Episcopal Day School, McAllen

Gorilla

THIRD GRAND PRIZE
FIRST PLACE, Mammals Division
FIRST PLACE, All Other Wild Mammals

Elena A. Mercado, Photographer
Glenda Rodriguez, Teacher
Dr. Americo Paredes School, Brownsville

Galapagos Tortoise

FOURTH GRAND PRIZE (tied)
FIRST PLACE, Reptiles & Amphibians Division
FIRST PLACE, Reptiles

Sarah M. Jesness, Photographer
Mrs. Flores, Teacher
Saint Anthony Catholic School, Diocese of Brownsville

Bluebonnets

FOURTH GRAND PRIZE (tied)
FIRST PLACE, Native Plants Division
FIRST PLACE, Grasses, Wildflowers

Vance J. Raders, Photographer
Mrs. Tankersly, Teacher
Saint John's Episcopal Day School, McAllen

Water Canal

FIRST PLACE, Waterways Division
FIRST PLACE, Man-made Waterways

Leslie M. Lewis, Photographer
Mrs. Tankersly, Teacher
Saint John's Episcopal Day School, McAllen

Geese

FIRST PLACE, Birds Division
FIRST PLACE, Shorebirds, Wading Birds & Waterfowl

Jonathan M. Burlette, Photographer
Mrs. Morfit, Teacher
Episcopal Day School, Brownsville

Swallowtail

FIRST PLACE, Insects & Arachnids Division
FIRST PLACE, Insects

William P. Wolfe, Photographer
Mrs. Morfit, Teacher
Episcopal Day School, Brownsville

ACKNOWLEDGMENTS

S P O N S O R S

THE VALLEY LAND FUND WILDLIFE PHOTO CONTEST

Our sponsors represent the heart of the contest, for it is through their generous funding that we are able to award the winning teams and acquire critical wildlife habitat. They are individuals, business owners and members of the community who love the outdoors and all the wildlife our brush country holds. We ask that you support the sponsors listed in the following pages, for they are the finest our communities have to offer. There would be no contest without their steadfast support and for that we are eternally greatful.

Special Acknowledgment

The Valley Land Fund holds all of its sponsors close to heart. Every contributor is instrumental in the success of the Wildlife Photo Contest. The organization would like to recognize and offer special gratitude to the Valley Chevy Dealers Association, Chevy Suburban, GMAC and The Nature Conservancy for their generous joint support of the South Texas Shootout. Together they are true champions of the chaparral.

SPONSOR OF THE YEAR

BOGGUS FORD

Boggus Ford has been a Grand Prize Sponsor of the Wildlife Photo Contest since the first event in 1994. When asked why, Frank Boggus says simply, "We believe in giving back to the community and we believe in what you are doing." The Boggus family came to the Valley early in the last century and has prospered in the automobile business. Giving back is part of their philosophy. Frank spearheaded the Harlingen Thicket project, where VLF and partners protected 40 acres in Harlingen, and has spent years making his own backyard "the smallest rainforest in the world." Frank's son, Bob, recognized the need to share the VLF contest photos with the public, and so he helped to instigate and market the first book, *Treasures of South Texas*. Frank and Bob Boggus believe the photo contests have inspired an excitement for nature and eco-tourism in the Valley that, in turn, has sparked the creation of nature festivals and added significant revenue to the Valley's economy. And that's good for business.

South Texas Shootout Sponsors

GRAND PRIZE
($5,000-15,000)
First Grand Prize
The Vannie Cook Award
Bentsen Palm Development
Rio Grande Regional Hospital
Texas State Bank
Boggus Motors
AEP/Central Power & Light

Second Grand Prize
The Argyle & Margaret McAllen Award
Knapp Medical Center

A. Clayton Scribner
Magic Valley Electric Co-op
Forest Oil Corporation
Alamo Bank of Texas
Jones & Cook Stationers
Payne Auto Group

Third Grand Prize
Wells Fargo
The Coneway Family Foundation

Fourth Grand Prize
The Loring Cook Foundation
Blockbuster Video
CopyZone

Mayfair Properties
Little Caesar's Pizza
NAI Rioco Realty

Fifth Grand Prize
JP Morgan Chase

Additional Grand Prize Sponsors
The Brownsville Herald
Frost National Bank
KGBT-TV Team 4 & Richard Moore
KRGV-TV Channel 5
KURV-710 Talk Radio
The Monitor
The Valley Morning Star

South Texas Shootout Sponsors (continued)

OFFICIAL SPONSORS ($5,000-35,000)
Official Vehicle - Chevy Suburban
Valley Chevy Dealers Association
General Motors/Chevy Suburban & The Nature Conservancy
General Motors Acceptance Corporation
Official Airport - McAllen Miller International Airport
Official Print Media - Freedom Communications
Official Car Rental Agency - Advantage Rent-A-Car

DIVISION SPONSORS ($3,000-5,000)
Charles Clark Chevrolet
Bill Burns
Amy & Kenneth Johnson
RGV Outdoors Center, Inc.
Shepard Walton King Insurance Group
Star of Texas Energy Services
Schaleben Limited Partnership
Tex-Best Travel Centers
Guerra Brothers in Honor of Rafael & Carmen Guerra

THE RARE CAT AWARD ($1,000-5,000)
Dora Valverde Fankhauser
John & Audrey Martin
D. Wilson Construction Company

CLASS SPONSORS ($1,000-3,000)
A.G. Edwards of McAllen
The Appraisal Company
Jeannie & Russell Barron
Mildred Erhart in Memory of Ted E. Erhart
Marsha Gamel Nelson, PhD - El Rocio
Kittleman, Thomas, Ramirez & Gonzales
Magnolia Charitable Trust
John & Audrey Martin
John & Judy McClung
Mobil Foundation, Inc.
Robert Townsend Trust
Santillana Ranch
Sheldon & Eve Weisfeld
Valley Insurance Services
Weyerhaueser Company Foundation

BEST OF CONTEST
Eagle Optics

ADDITIONAL SUPPORT
Fin 2 Feathers
Lauren G. Johnson & Family
Laurie & Jibber Terhaggen

Small Tract Competition Sponsors

GRAND PRIZE SPONSORS ($1,000-3,000)
Bushnell Sports Optics
Eagle Optics
CopyZone
B & H Photo-Video
Carol Rausch
Burton Auto Supply, Inc.
Pete & Vicki Moore
Mother Nature's Creations
Weyerhaeuser Company Foundation

DIVISION SPONSORS ($500-1,000)
Cynthia Little Allen Memorial
Ruth Martin Memorial
Office Furniture U.S.A.
Dr. William Peck Memorial

CLASS SPONSORS ($100-500)
Linda & Wes Johnson
Carroll E. & June Elliott
Bob Stelzer & Mike Heep
A. Clayton Scribner Memorial
Fin 2 Feathers
J.N. Vertrees Memorial

ADDITIONAL SUPPORT
Anna Belle Mayo Memorial
Gateway Printing & Office Supply
Luby's Restaurant (McAllen North)
Risto Heikkinen Memorial
Agnes Kathley Memorial
Don Pye Memorial
Hollis Rankin Memorial
Terry Wilsher Memorial
Frances L. Wilson Memorial
Anne West Memorial

Youth Photo Contest Sponsors

GRAND PRIZE SPONSOR ($10,000)
Robert Townsend

DIVISION SPONSORS ($500-1000)
Copy Zone
Johnson Brothers Construction

BEST OF CONTEST SPONSOR ($100-500)
Hunt's Photo & Video

PARTICIPATING PHOTOGRAPHERS

These photographers make a tremendous commitment of time, money, blood, sweat and tears to create the images you see in this book. They are pushed to perform to a level beyond what most would consider humanly possible, thus the contest's nickname, the "iron man contest."

Following are the photographers in alphabetical order, as well as their home towns, states and countries.

SOUTH TEXAS SHOOTOUT

Cathy Allinder
Virginia Beach, VA

Charles Anderson
McAllen, TX

David Armstrong
Richmond, TX

Juan E. Bahamón
Corpus Christi, TX

Barbara Baird
Lockport, IL

Don Bartram
Albuquerque, NM

Ken Beard
Spring, TX

David & Mary Bechtol
Canyon, TX

Richard Beeckman
Saginaw, MI

Steve Bentsen
McAllen, TX

Lynn Bieber-Weir & Ray Bieber
McAllen, TX

Jerry J. Box
McAllen, TX

Bill Burns
McAllen, TX

Jim & Deva Burns
Scottsdale, AZ

Bill Carter
Church Hill, TN

Bill Caskey
Austin, TX

Dominique & Dwight Chamberlain
Driggs, ID

Richard Day
Alma, IL

Don Dean
Houston, TX

Michael Delesantro
Weslaco, TX

Vern Denman
McAllen, TX

Larry Ditto
McAllen, TX

Mary Donahue
Harlingen, TX

Bill Draker
San Antonio, TX

Randall Ennis
McAllen, TX

Dennis Erhart
Santa Fe, NM

Sean Fitzgerald
Dallas, TX

Eddie & Alta Forshage
McAllen, TX

Manuel S. Garcia
Sarita, TX

Omar Garcia
Austin, TX

Pedro Garcia
Linn, TX

Alberto Gutíerrez
Edinburg, TX

Derrick Hamrick & Roberta E. Summers
Raleigh, NC

Jay Hardy
Madisonville, TX

Julieanne Harris
Philadelphia, PA

Mark Harvey
Aspen, CO

Glenn Hayes
Markham, TX

Joseph Holman
Brownsville, TX

Don Jackson
Forestville, CA

Mary Jo Janovsky
Harlingen, TX

Gary Kramer
Willows, CA

Fred LaBounty
Harker Heights, TX

Kermit Denver Laird
Starkville, MS

Marilyn Moseley LaMantia & Angela Reine LaMantia,
Edinburg, TX

Greg W. Lasley
Austin, TX

J. Stephen Lay
Corpus Christi, TX

Ike Leahy
Gresham, OR

Hugh Lieck
Kingsville, TX

Vance D. MacDonald
Las Vegas, NV

Thomas D. Mangelsen
Jackson, WY

Downs Matthews
Houston, TX

Gary & Christine McHale
Richmond Hill, Ontario
Canada

Laura Elaine Moore
McAllen, TX

David A. Murray
Southport, ME

Merrill Nix
Artesia, NM

Rolf Nussbaumer
Oberägeri, Switzerland

Richard B. Parker
Brownsville, TX

Don Pederson
Tomball, TX

Linda F. Peterson
Ventura, CA

John Pickles
Barataria, LA

David Powel
Albuquerque, NM

Wallace Prukop
San Benito, TX

Irene Hinke-Sacilotto
Joppa, MD

George & Linda Sangrik
Hudson, OH

Bob Simpson
McAllen, TX

Joseph V. Smith
Houston, TX

Clay Thurston
Knoxville, TN

John & Gloria Tveten
Baytown, TX

Tom Urban
Falfurrias, TX

Martin & Ester Volpe
McAllen, TX

Sharon Waite
Mission, TX

Jack C. Watson, Justice (Rtd.)
Lake Charles, LA

Dave Welling
Canoga Park, CA

Mark & Sue Werner
Rock Falls, IL

Jeremy Woodhouse
The Colony, TX

SMALL TRACT COMPETITION

Catalina Grace Bacod
Rio Grande City, TX

Brian Barber
Pharr, TX

Taylor Blanton
San Benito, TX

Jim Bush
McAllen, TX

Zandra M. Cantú
McAllen

Alberto X. Chapa, Sr.
Mission, TX

Esperanza S. Chapa
McAllen, TX

Hector Chapa
Mission, TX

Hunter Cofoid
McAllen, TX

Scarlet & George Colley
South Padre Island, TX

Joe Corso
McAllen, TX

Tony & Joshua Corso
McAllen, TX

Audrie S. Crane
McAllen, TX

Fortunato Del Angel
Mexico

Jean Domansi
Rio Grande City, TX

Carla M. Ellard
San Marcos, TX

Dr. Lucile Estell
Rockdale, TX

Ted A. Falls, Jr.
Alamo, TX

Rafa Flores
McAllen, TX

Mark Glazer
McAllen, TX

John Harris
Edinburg, TX

J.D. Hensz
McAllen, TX

Rex Hewitt
Laguna Vista, TX

Lowell Hudsonpillar
Mission, TX

Kenneth & Amy Johnson
McAllen, TX

Ariel King
Mission, TX

Rajnish Kumar
Houston, TX

Vinod Kumar
Houston, TX

Rosa Linda Lashbrook
Rio Hondo, TX

Bill Leidner
Mission, TX

Miguel S. López
Rio Grande City, TX

Johnny Martinez
Pharr, TX

Daniel A. Montelongo Lugo
Reynosa, Tamps. México

Mary Frances Noell
Progreso Lakes, TX

Jimmy Paz
Brownsville, TX

Patty Raney
Harlingen, TX

Manuel Rodriguez, Jr.
Rio Grande City, TX

Sally Ross
Mercedes, TX

Victor E. Sanchez
McAllen, TX

Steve Sinclair
Brownsville, TX

Rob & Susan Stevenson
McAllen, TX

Bryan & Linh Thiel
Houston, TX

Charles Vieh
San Benito, TX

Carlos J. Villarreal
Brownsville, TX

Antonio Vindell
Brownsville, TX

Cara E. Wade
South Padre Island, TX

Don Wiley
San Benito, TX

Lee Zieger
Brownsville, TX

YOUTH PHOTO CONTEST

Samantha Barnett
McAllen, TX

Nicole M. Bradford
Mercedes, TX

Victoria Jeanne Cammack
McAllen, TX

LyLony Cazares
Weslaco, TX

Stephanie Chavez
McAllen, TX

Philip Cofoid
McAllen, TX

Trevor Cofoid
McAllen, TX

Blaine Davis
Corpus Christi, TX

Vonda Denny
Harlingen, TX

Kevin Ryan Doyle
Mission, TX

Blake Eikenhorst
Brenham, TX

John David Franz, Jr.
McAllen, TX

Omar Gamez
McAllen, TX

Rick Gamez
McAllen, TX

Karel Garcia
Mission, TX

Liliana Gomez
Brownsville, TX

Josh Harris
Edinburg, TX

Erin M. Holland
Mission, TX

Katie Holland
Mission, TX

Lauren G. Johnson
San Antonio, TX

Erin Keelin
Port Isabel, TX

Charlene Kroeker
McAllen, TX

Mario Louis Leal
Harlingen, TX

Stephen Leidner
Mission, TX

Jeremy W. Lewis
Combes, TX

Lauren Ashley Link
Mission, TX

Michael Anthony Luna
Edinburg, TX

Sidney S. Meadows
McAllen, TX

Richard T. Moore
San Benito, TX

Schuyler Moore
San Benito, TX

Greg Moran
San Benito, TX

Sydney Anne Noser
McAllen, TX

Cassie Patton
Mission, TX

Faith Patton
Mission, TX

Vanessa Pilarczyk
Edinburg, TX

Stephen Rispoli
Brownsville, TX

Analisa Rodriguez
Brownsville, TX

Kevin Michael Rodríguez
Santa Rosa, TX

Robin Kimberly Rodríguez
Santa Rosa, TX

Vicky Rodriguez
Linn, TX

Catherine Saenz
McAllen, TX

Codi Sellers
McAllen, TX

Crystal Simpson
McAllen, TX

Sarah Stenseng
Harlingen, TX

Erica Ann Vasquez
Harlingen, TX

PARTICIPATING LANDOWNERS

Private landowners play a crucial role in the conservation of wildlife today and we applaud their efforts. Without their participation in conservation, entire ecosystems may be lost, never to be appreciated by future generations.

Following are the participants in alphabetical order, as well as the county or city of the property.

SOUTH TEXAS SHOOTOUT

Mary N. Baldridge
Starr

Cleve & Rosemary Breedlove
Inn at Chachalaca Bend
Los Fresnos

William Richard Buchholz
Starr, Zapata

Monica & Ray Burdette
El Canelo Ranch
Kenedy

Bill Burns / Bill Burns Ranch
Hidalgo

Ramiro & Mari Caballero
Brooks

Camp Lula Sams
Cameron

A. Cantú Farms
Hidalgo, Jim Hogg,
Starr, Willacy

Cap Rock Pens
Eddie & Alta Forshage
Hidalgo

Joe E. Chapa Family Ranch
San Manuel

Colima Ranch
Cameron

Jim & Kathy Collins
Cook Ranches
Starr, Hidalgo

CM Cozad Ranch
Hidalgo

David & Lois Day
    George & June Toland
San Cristobal Ranch
Starr

Daniel Drefke
Skipper Ranch
Brooks

Rafael Flores Ranch
Zapata

Dr. Martín & Celia Garcia
Hacienda La Esperanza
Willacy

El Devisadero Ranch
Miguel A. &
    Analicia Q. Garcia
Kenedy

David & Diane Garza
El Monte del Rancho Viejo
Cameron

Pat & Amy Ginsbach,
    Chris & Wayne
    Westphal
Palm Gardens, Inc.
Hidalgo

Gerry & Martha Glick
Brooks

Guerra Brothers
Hidalgo, Starr

Douglas Hardie
Cameron

King Ranch, Inc.
Brooks, Kenedy

Krenmueller Farms
Bert & Trudy Forthuber
Hidalgo

C.W. Helling
La Mota Ranch
Jim Hogg

Las Majadas Ranch
Winifred Wetegrove
Willacy

Conley Ranch,
Carla Conley
    & Kenneth Mark Haynes
Willacy

Lebh Shomea House of Prayer
La Parra Ranch
Kenedy

Dr. Ford & Jackie Lockett
    and Mary Lib &
    Bill McManus
Cameron

The Mary B. Ranch
Bill & Mary Bertha Mallet
Kenedy, Willacy

John and Audrey Martin
Hidalgo

Margaret & Robert McAllen
Las Colmenas Ranch
Hidalgo

McAllen Properties
Hidalgo, Starr

Minten Ranch
Brooks

The Nature Conservancy
Cameron, Hidalgo

El Negro Ranch
Barry & Elizabeth Roberts
Starr

Payne Ranch
Kenedy

Pérez Ranch
Hidalgo

RGV Outdoors Center, Inc.
Mary Jo & Mike Janovsky
Cameron

Rio Grande Container Game Ranch
Harold Jones & Mark Gibbs, Owners
Starr

San Pedro Ranch
Baldo & Danny Vela
Hidalgo

Schaleben Ranch
Hidalgo

Speer Ranch
Juanita Farley, Owner
Darrell & Suzie Thompson,
    Managers
Starr

Starr Feedyard
Starr, Hidalgo

Joseph & Betty Lou Sutton /
Sutton Ranches
Jim Hogg, Willacy

El Tecolote Ranch
Phil & Karen Hunke
Hidalgo

Tecomate Ranch Partners
Hidalgo, Jim Hogg, Starr

Varal Ranches, Ltd.
Martin Volpe, Jr.
Zapata

Waite/Metz Farm
Hidalgo

Steve Walker /
Phillips Ranch, Inc. Team
Cameron

Weaver Ranch
Ken & Barbara,
Kent & G'Anne
Willacy

H. Yturria Ranch
Kenedy

Roberto & Fran Yzaguirre
Rancho Yzaguirre
Starr, Jim Hogg

SMALL TRACT COMPETITION

Ernest Aliseda
Edinburg

Martha Russell Blanton,
Los Ebanos Preserve
San Benito

Lisa & Steve Cofoid
McAllen

Cohrs Ranch
Jon Cohrs
Donna

Corso Family Properties
McAllen

Charles J. Ellard, Homestead
Edinburg

Frontera Audubon Society Center,
Weslaco Thicket & Museum
Weslaco

Joe Hamilton
San Benito

John & Jeanine Harris
Brooks, Hidalgo

Shawn W. Horton,
Rancho El Javaline
Alamo

Kenneth & Amy Johnson
McAllen

Barbara L. Kennett
South Padre Island

Todd Lashbrook
Paso Real Farm
Rio Hondo

López Ranch
Miguel S. López
Zapata

Johnny Martinez
Pharr

James & Georgiana Matz,
Cielo Escondido
Cameron

Marsha Gamel Nelson,
El Rocio
Mission

Robert & Martha Noell,
Homesite
Progreso Lakes

George Powell &
Ariel King
Mission

Rancho Lomitas
Benito & Toni Treviño
Rio Grande City

C.L. & Patty Raney
Harlingen

Resaca Grove Farm
Brownsville

Rio Viejo-J.D. Hensz
Cameron

Manuel Rodriguez, Jr.,
Rodriguez Properties
Rio Grande City

Ross Family
Mercedes

Sabal Palm Audubon
Center & Sanctuary
Cameron

Santa Rita Ranch
Mission

AV Shull Properties
Hidalgo

Trev & Donna Jo Sparks
McAllen

TCAP
La Feria

Vieh's Bed & Breakfast
San Benito

Arnoldo Villarreal
Brownsville

Antonio & Sharon Vindell
Brownsville

Saints of the Chaparral

Book patrons, along with sponsors of prizes in the contest, are the patron saints of The Valley Land Fund. Over one hundred individuals and businesses have agreed to buy from 20 to 250 or more of this current book. Such a vote up front allows the VLF to move forward with production of the book, ensuring the printing costs and serving as a huge encouragement to those VLF members charged with producing and marketing the book. It also shows the confidence that these bulk buyers have in the quality of the books, which they distribute as gifts to their family, friends, business associates, and clientele.

This material witness of the book patrons serves another important purpose. It reminds the world that successful people may also be cogent believers in the importance of preserving wildlife habitat. As chairman of the book patrons drive, I must admit that it was only a few years ago that I realized how important it is to develop effective stewardship of our natural resources. I did not understand the complexity of the dance of life before my very eyes until my friend Neal King, Jr. took me for a ride through the gentle hills, brush, and grasslands of a Valley ranch. He pointed out plants and animals whose stories I had never heard. As Neal explained how things worked in the chaparral, I began to truly enjoy the brushland for the first time in my life.

Here in the Valley, the mystery of life is everywhere around us. Our participation is an adventure into what is important in life, gifts to be shared and cared for with family and friends as well as newcomers. The chaparral must be preserved, cherished for its own innate worthiness, as well as its ability to refocus us on what is really our connection to our Source.

That is why I claim our book patrons as patron saints. By ensuring the viability of the books, book patrons furnish the resources that can then be leveraged for the benefit of all citizens of South Texas. With the proceeds from book sales, The Valley Land Fund can move forward in its work of preservation. And as this beautiful book is opened and perused in schools, homes and businesses, the solemn duty to our surroundings is imprinted on the minds and hearts of those who come after us, that is, the future patron saints of the chaparral.

By the uncommon and courageous support of our patrons and sponsors, we are able to make known through the testimony of photography what is sacred to our land—the critters, their mystery and the beauty that surrounds them.

–Kirk Clark, Chairman, Book Patron Committee

Photographer: Rolf Nussbaumer / Landowner: Rio Grande Container Game Ranch

PHOTO BOOK PATRONS

250 or more books
Rio Grande Regional Hospital
Santa Fe Ranch
Valley Baptist Health Systems

100 or more
Chase Bank of Texas
Knapp Medical Center
The Loring Cook Foundation
Rio Grande Container Game Ranch,
  Harold Jones & Mark Gibbs
Sierra Title
The Monitor

50 or more
The Brownsville Herald
Clark Chevrolet, Kirk & Jeri Clark
CopyZone
Gateway Printing & Office Supply, Inc.
Hollon Oil
McAllen Chamber of Commerce
Security Land Title
Shepard Walton King Insurance Group
Texas State Bank

40 or more
Guerra Brothers Successors LTD
Inn at Chachalaca Bend
Jones & Cook Stationers
San Pedro Ranch, Baldo & Danny Vela
Sierra Title Company of Cameron
  and Willacy Counties
Frank Smith Toyota
Lynne Tate Real Estate
Tipotex Chevrolet, Inc.

30 or more
Boggus Ford
Children's Dental Center,
  Dr. Phil & Karen Hunke
Descon Construction, L.P.
Harlingen Area Chamber of Commerce
McAllen National Bank
Pete & Vicki Moore
Payne Auto Group
Walker & Twenhafel, L.L.P.
Stephan & Eryn Wingert

20 or more
Alamo Bank of Texas
Am-Mex Products
Arroyo Reds
Artline & Masterpiece Cafe
Ballenger Construction
Britton's Photo Imaging
L.T. Boswell
Boultinghouse Simpson Architects
Dennis Burleson, A.G. Edwards & Sons
Burton Companies
Broadway Hardware & Gifts
Cactus Flower
Cardenas Auto Group
Bob Carter, Blue Fusion Design
Cinch Connectors de Mexico
Clark Knapp Honda
Las Colmenas Ranch
Rip Davenport & Associates
Greg Douglas, A.G. Edwards & Sons
Echo Hotel
Edinburg Chamber of Commerce
Edwards Abstract and Title Co.

A.G. Edwards & Sons, Brownsville
Ellis, Koeneke & Ramirez, LLP
Enterprise Rent-A-Car
Foremost Paving, Inc., Alta & Eddie Forshage
Friends of the Wildlife Corridor
Greater Mission Chamber of Commerce
Art & Barbara Guerra
Hart, Silva & Company
Carla C. & Kenneth M. Haynes
Jim & Karen Henderson
Hidalgo County Historical Society
Larry T. & Mary Jane Hunter
Images for Conservation Fund
Inland Paperboard & Packaging, Inc.
International Bank of Commerce and
  Bill Martin, A.G. Edwards
InterNational Bank
JS Media, LLC
Kellogg Chevrolet Inc.
Dorothy & Neal King
Kittleman, Thomas, Ramirez
  & Gonzales, P.L.L.C.
Kiwanis Club of Edinburg
Knapp Chevrolet
Kreidler Funeral Home Inc.
Lone Star National Bank
Long, Chilton LLP of Brownsville
Long, Chilton LLP of McAllen
Cullen & Carol Lynn Looney
John & Dottie Malcom
Marleen's Hall
John & Audrey Martin
City of McAllen
McAllen Economic Development Corp.

Judy & John McClung and
  Martha Russell & Taylor Blanton
Charlie & Virginia Meyer
Pat & Beverly Moody
Mother Nature's Creations
Pat Moyer
Myrgv.com
Naturally Curious, Inc., Randy Mock
Marsha & Dan Nelson
Miguel A. Nevarez, President,
  The University of Texas Pan-American
Nuevo Santander Gallery
Bert Ogden
Steve & Flora Parr
Joe & Shawn Patterson
Pharr Chamber of Commerce
Photo Craft Laboratories
John & Lica Pinkston
Carol Rausch
Rio Bank
Rio Grande Valley Outdoors Center
Bill & Susie Robertson
Jim & Donna Rowland
Russell Plantation
Santa Cecilia Ranch
Schaleben Limited Partnership
Service Group
Frank & Helen Shepard
Steve & Suzanne Shepard
Smith, Fankhauser, Voight & Watson
Dr. Oscar Sotelo
South Texas Community College
Southern Texas Title Company
Trev & Donna Jo Sparks
Speer Ranch, Juanita Farley,

Darrell & Suzie Thompson
Spence Concrete Co.
Spikes Ford
Sandra Sweeney Wilson
Molly Thornberry
Tipton Motors, Inc.
T.N.T. Photo and Patty Raney
Unomedical
Tom Urban
The University of Texas Pan-American
  Foundation
Valley International Airport
Valley Nature Center
Valley Mortgage Company, Inc.
Van Burkleo Motors
Roscoe & Betty Watkins
Weyerhaeuser Paper Company
Linda & James Williams
Williamson Construction Co.
Windows of Nature, by Dee An Pederson
World Birding Center

Photo Book Patron Committee

Kirk Clark, Chairman
April Cuellar
Nancy Dooley
Bill Elliott
Paula Flores
Carla & Kenneth Haynes
Ruth Hoyt
Karen Hunke
Neal King
Wes Kittleman
John Martin
Christina Martinez

Judy McClung
Carol Rausch
Mark & Teresa Roberts
Bob Simpson
Cody Sparks & Michele Sparks
Randy Sweeten
Lew Vassberg
Danny Vela
Eryn Reddell Wingert & Stephan Wingert

Photographer: Victor E. Sanchez
Landowner: Marsha Gamel Nelson / El Rocio

PHOTO BOOK COMMITTEE & CONTRIBUTORS

Committee Members

Eryn Reddell Wingert, Editor & Chairman
Ruth Hoyt, Co-Editor & Photo Contest Director
Jan Seale, Copy Editor
Lynn Bieber-Weir
David Cantú
Kirk Clark
Mark Gibbs
Ariel King
Audrey G. Martin
John Martin, V.P. Photo Contest
Judy McClung, V.P. Photo Contest

Contributors

IDENTIFICATION CONSULTANTS

John Arvin
Robert Behrstock
David Blankinship
Pat Burchfield
Mike Carlo
Carrie Cate
David Martin
John McClung
Mike Quinn

WRITERS
Kirk Clark
Ruth Hoyt

Audrey G. Martin
Richard Moore
Elizabeth Pierson
Jan Seale
Ron Smith
Eryn Reddell Wingert

DESIGN AND LAYOUT
CopyZone, Tony Corso
Esperanza S. Chapa
Leonel Cantú

PRINTING COORDINATION
AND COLOR WORK
Blue Fusion Design, Bob Carter

PRINTER
Gateway Printing & Office Supply, Inc.,
Lin Miller

ORGANIZATION AND SUPPORT
Belle Cedillo
Ruth Hoyt, Photo Contest Director
Merritt Hunke
Sam Mason, Assistant Photo Contest Director
Lin Miller
Myra Pérez

The Valley Land Fund
Wildlife Photo Books

Spirit of the Chaparral is the fifth Valley Land Fund wildlife photo book. This book follows in the tradition of displaying amazing images and the stories behind them. *Spirit of the Chaparral* carries on the legacy of promoting conservation and preservation.

Treasures of South Texas (1995)
Creatures on the Edge (1997)
The Lens and the Land (1999)
Focus on the Wild (2001)
Spirit of the Chaparral (2003)

2002 BOARD OF DIRECTORS

The Valley Land Fund

Mission Statement

To preserve, expand and enhance the native wildlife habitat in the Rio Grande Valley through education, land ownership and creation of economic incentives for preservation.

BOARD OFFICERS
Cleve Breedlove, President
John Martin, V.P.-Photo Contest
Judy McClung, V.P.-Photo Contest
Larry Ditto, V.P.-Land Preservation
Wes Kittleman, Treasurer
Alice G.K.K. East, Secretary
Neal King, Past-President

BOARD MEMBERS
Rosemary Breedlove
Christine Yturria Buford
William Burns
Kirk Clark
Tony Corso
Jim Deuser
Oscar Garcia
Karen Hunke
Dr. Phil Hunke
Amy Johnson
Jane Kittleman
Jackie Lockett
Cullen Looney

John Malcom, Jr.
Virginia Meyer
Pat Moody
Hal Morrow
Susanne J. Robertson
Wayne Showers
Bob Simpson
Ellen Stone
Lynne Tate
Fran Yzaguirre

ADVISORY BOARD
Dennis Burleson
Michael Delesantro
Evelyn East
Bill Elliott
A.R. (Felo) Guerra
Dr. Marla Guerra
Melissa Guerra
Carla Haynes
Piper Montemayor
Bud Payne
Librada (Libby) Perez

Jan Seale
Ron Smith
Nancy Stafford
Allen Williams

HONORARY BOARD
Joe Charles Ballenger
Dr. Steve Bentsen
Dr. Don Farst
Mark Feldman
Dr. Juliet Garcia
Jack Hart
Kevin Hiles
Bill Hollon
Tom Koeneke
Audrey G. Martin
James A. McAllen
T. Edward Mercer
Pete Moore
Carol Rausch
Dr. Gary M. Schwarz
Frank Yturria

Afterword

The child eagerly climbs the worn stairs to the musty attic of his grandparents. It is a daily ritual of curiosity. He arrives in semi-darkness to the sight of scattered piles of books. He slides a large book from one of the dusty stacks and sits hunched forward on the floor. Minimal light slants through the small windows onto the pages that he spreads across his knees.

The book-of-the-day shows him another world bright with color in contrast with his sanctuary. As he turns the glossy pages, the scenes upon them make him smile, but there are also frowns. What are these creatures illuminating the paper? When and where did they dwell? The scarlet birds that flash out at him in almost three dimensions. The mottled butterfly that appears to vibrate against the green foliage. The spotted cat staring at him, frozen in the moment of wariness and indecision. The two deer rising in boxers' poses against the red sunset. A bright green katydid straddling branches.

The child's expression is quizzical. He raises his head and looks out the window to the murky horizon where high buildings rise bleak and lifeless. What contrast with the crystal-clear images in the book!

At that moment, only five miles away beyond the city at a brushland waterhole, a Vermilion bird with dark wings perches on a Golden Huisache tree, alert to movement in the air about him. He sallies out, snaps an insect in mid-flight and returns to the tree. Below, Whistling-Ducks and White Waders decorate the pond–a leathery blue-black snake coils on the bank. And there is no discordant sound of the city. . . only the pleasant traffic of Nature.

They are still here, the creatures of the pages. They WILL NOT exist in mere memory. Some day the child will believe that people with foresight chose to preserve what might have been lost only to the realm of dusty books.

The child in all of us CAN descend the attic stairs and find those scenes. Like children we play every day with the future. Let us play wisely.

–Ron Smith

Photographer: Sean Fitzgerald & Jeremy Woodhouse / Landowner: Roberto & Fran Yzaguirre

PHOTOGRAPHER & LANDOWNER INDEX

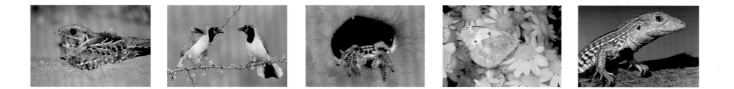